Adoption

and

Ethics

A SERIES BY MADELYN FREUNDLICH

THE MARKET FORCES IN ADOPTION

CHILD WELFARE LEAGUE OF AMERICA
THE EVAN B. DONALDSON ADOPTION INSTITUTE

The Child Welfare League of America (CWLA), the nation's oldest and largest membership-based child welfare organization, is committed to engaging all Americans in promoting the well-being of children and protecting every child from harm.

CHILD WELFARE LEAGUE OF AMERICA, INC.
440 First Street, NW, Third Floor
Washington, DC 20001-2085
E-mail: books@cwla.org

CURRENT PRINTING (last digit)
10 9 8 7 6 5 4 3 2 1

Cover design by James D. Melvin
Text design by Peggy Porter Tierney

Printed in the United States of America
ISBN # 0-87868-913-3

Library of Congress Cataloging-in-Publication Data
Freundlich, Madelyn.
    The market forces in adoption/by Madelyn Freundlich.
        p.   cm.
    Includes bibliographical references.
    ISBN 0-87868-913-3
    1. Adoption--Economic aspects--United States. 2. Adoption--
        United States--Finance.
    I. Title

HV875.55.F73 2000
362.73'4'0973--dc21

00-063878

Contents

Preface

This volume is the second in a series of publications developed by the Evan B. Donaldson Adoption Institute and published by CWLA Press. The series is part of the Adoption Institute's multiyear initiative focused on ethical issues in adoption. It is designed to provide the field with a synthesis of the current base of knowledge on key adoption policy and practice issuesVissues that currently pose challenges to adoption professionals and which are likely to confront the field in the future. This volume on the market forces in adoption follows an earlier published volume on the role of race, culture, and national origin in adoption. Forthcoming volumes will focus on the impact of adoption on members of the adoption triad, and adoption and the reproductive technologies.

Why a Focus on Ethics in Adoption

Adoption is a complex subject, with social, psychological, legal, and cultural dimensions. It is shaped by policy—at the international, national, state, county and agency levels—and by practice—on the part of social workers, attorneys, judges, mental health professionals, and others. It involves the needs, interests, and rights of children, birth parents, relatives, foster parents, adoptive parents, and adult adoptees. Adoption includes domestic adoptions of healthy newborns, international adoptions of children from dozens of countries with widely varying policies, and adoptions of children in foster care in this country. Because of this complexity, adoption has been and continues to be the subject of much debate. The controversies in adoption have extended across a spectrum of policy and practice issues, and although the contentious issues have become clear, resolution has not been achieved nor has consensus developed regarding a framework on which to further quality adoption policy and practice.

Productive outcomes have been hindered by the constituency-based considerations that have shaped, to a great extent, the tenor of the debate. Emotion and rhetoric have come to characterize much of the discussion and, as a result, it has been difficult to focus on substantive issues in a reasoned and informed manner or clarify the goals and principles that can assist in resolving the many points of disagreement. From the divisive debates on access to identifying information, to the emotionally-laden controversies on transracial adoption, to the increasingly intense disputes over the competing "rights" of members of the adoption triad—the environment surrounding adoption has become highly charged and focused efforts to craft quality policy and practice more difficult to achieve.

The Adoption Institute, in collaboration with leading thinkers in the field of adoption from across the country, approached this environment by proposing an ethics-based framework for analyzing and resolving the complex challenges in adoption. The decision to utilize an ethics-based approach was based, first, on a belief that ethics could provide a method for reframing the critical issues in adoption and avoiding the divisiveness that has impeded the resolution of the key challenges. Second, the choice of an ethics-based approach was based on an assessment that such a framework would support the identification of the range of issues that impact contemporary adoption, the analysis of relevant considerations from multiple perspectives, and the development of a course of action for improving future policy and practice. The Adoption Institute's ethics initiative has three major components:

- an identification and examination of the core values and principles that underlie quality adoption policy and practice;

- thorough analyses of the critical policy and practice issues that demand attention; and

- the development of a strategy that draws on a sound knowledge base to advance quality adoption policy and practice in the future.

The Critical Issues in Adoption

Because adoption is complex, bringing to the fore many competing interests, values, perspectives, and constituencies, it is not an easy task to reach consensus on which issues represent the most critical questions. The Adoption Institute approached this challenging process by first bringing together a multidisciplinary Ethics Advisory Committee. The members of this group represent a rich diversity of professional backgrounds and expertise, including adoption practice and policy, clinical psychology, sociology, political science, the law, the judiciary, bioethics, medicine, medical anthropology, religion, and social science research. With the guidance of this Committee, the Adoption Institute identified key ethical issues that affect adoption policy and practice and prioritized the most critical issues for in depth analysis and action. The following topics were selected as critical areas for ongoing attention and work:

The Role of Race, Culture, and National Origin in Adoption

This topic—on which a previous volume focused—considers critical questions regarding the role of race, culture and national origin in adoption from the perspective of individuals served by adoption and from a broad policy perspective. In this complex area of adoption policy and practice, there are many unresolved questions related to the role of race, culture and national origin in an adoptee's personal identity and the extent to which racial and cultural similarities and differences between adoptive parents and children should be taken into account. These questions have been placed at the forefront of the policy debate as a result of recent changes in federal law—which now prohibits consideration of race and culture in the adoptive placement of children in foster care; debates related to the Indian Child Welfare Act; and the mandates of the Hague Convention on Intercountry Adoption.

The Impact of Adoption on Adopted Persons, Birth Parents, Adoptive Parents, and Adoptive Families

This topic focuses on the many ways that adoption may impact each member of the adoption triad. For the adopted person, adoption may affect the individual's overall adjustment and well-being, as well as the ability to develop a personal identity. What are the outcomes for adopted persons, and to what extent do past and current adoption practices affect those outcomes? For the birth parent, adoption practice and law may impact, both in the short and long term, an individual's sense of personal integrity. To what extent are birth parents well served by adoption and how do societal perceptions of birth parents affect their sense of well-being? For adoptive parents, adoption involves achieving parenthood in a non-traditional way. To what extent does being "approved" to parent impact adoptive parents? Do adoptive families face special challenges in a society that accords primacy to biological bonds?

The Market Forces in Adoption

This topic—the focus of this volume—considers various aspects of the "business" of adoption in terms of market factors. With the shifting demographics of infant adoption, international adoption, and special needs adoption, issues are raised about the role of money in adoption, who holds the "power" in adoption, and to whom adoption professionals are accountable. Increasingly, the field of adoption struggles with such questions as: To what extent has there been a commodification of children who are placed with adoptive families? How is the adoption process regulated and by whom? How are the roles of birth and adoptive parents affected by differences in resources? Is the concept of accountability relevant to adoption, and if so, how? Do market forces undermine ethical adoption practice?

Adoption and Reproductive Technology

This fourth topic raises the question of whether reproductive technologies (including sperm donation, egg donation, and embryo implantation), which may or may not provide a child genetically connected to one or both parents, create a situation that is analogous to adoption. Should the knowledge that has been acquired in the field of adoption be applied in the area of reproductive technologies? Are issues in adoption—such as identity, access to background information, and search—equally applicable in the context of reproductive technology? Should any or all adoption practice standards apply in reproductive technologies?

The Series

Essential to knowledgeable discussion and issue resolution in each of these four areas is a sound understanding of the current knowledge base—the research, the practice-based knowledge, and the policy analyses advanced by leading thinkers in the many fields bearing on adoption: social work, law, psychology, child and adolescent development, medicine, and education. The volumes are designed to provide a synthesis of the existing knowledge base that can inform and challenge thinking and analysis in each of the critical topic areas. They outline the key issues; review the current data, including statistical information to the extent it exists; identify the research that addresses the key issues; describe the current practice-based knowledge; and synthesize the policy arguments that have been advanced and debated. Whenever possible, the strengths and weaknesses of various perspectives are assessed.

The series, including this volume on market forces in adoption, is not designed to take a position on the issues or advance a specific viewpoint as to what is "ethical" or "unethical." It is only through ongoing discussion that consensus can be reached as to what represents the most ethical course of action in adoption—for those directly touched by adoption and for those who provide professional adoption services. It is hoped that the volume series will provide a tool for furthering this discussion—a springboard for advancing adoption policy and practice currently and into the future.

Madelyn Freundlich
The Evan B. Donaldson Adoption Institute

Acknowledgments

The Evan B. Donaldson Adoption Institute acknowledges a number of individuals who provided assistance in the development of this publication on the market forces in adoption. The following individuals generously gave of their time and expertise in reviewing drafts and offered critical guidance and suggestions: Roger Bouwma, Director of International Services, Bethany Christian Services, Grand Rapids, MI; Susan Soon-Keum Cox, Vice President of Public Policy & External Affairs, Holt International Children's Services, Eugene, OR; Dr. Dixie Davis, Executive Director, The Adoption Exchange, Aurora, CO; James Gritter, Child Welfare Supervisor, Catholic Human Services, Traverse City, MI; Michelle Hester, Director, International Adoption Program, The Barker Foundation, Cabin John, MD; Barbara Holtan, Director of Adoption Services, Tressler Lutheran Services, York, PA; Professor Ruth-Arlene W. Howe, Boston College Law School, Newton Centre, MA; Ann Sullivan, former Director of Adoption Services, Child Welfare League of America, Washington, DC; and Jake Terpstra, former Child Welfare Services Specialist, U.S. Children's Bureau, Grand Rapids, MI.

The research assistance of Demetra Kasimis and the editorial assistance of Leigh Nowicki, Program Assistant at The Evan B. Donaldson Adoption Institute, are also gratefully acknowledged. Ms. Kasimis' research and Ms. Nowicki's ongoing support and expertise were essential to the completion of this monograph.

Introduction

One of the most compelling issues confronting the field of adoption today is the extent to which market forces are shaping practice and policy. There are critical questions about the role that money is playing in adoption, who holds power in the context of adoption decision-making, and to what extent there is accountability to those whose lives are touched by adoption. The themes of money, power, and accountability arise in the adoption of infants in the United States, international adoption, and the adoption of children in foster care in this country. This volume considers each of these three major forms of adoption in relation to market forces and the role of marketing in adoption—by prospective adoptive parents and by adoption professionals. It raises a number of ethical questions in relation to market forces as they currently impact adoption practice and policy, and the effect that these forces are likely to have in the future.

Part I

Market Forces: The Adoption of Infants in the United States

With the declining availability of healthy white newborns for adoption [Sokoloff 1993] and the increased demand for infants as infertility rates have risen [Abma et al. 1997], the imbalance between supply and demand has become more apparent. The growing numbers of individuals seeking to adopt an infant in this country face an increasingly competitive environment because of the diminished supply of infants, and, in accordance with general economic principles, costs associated with adoption have risen. In both agency adoptions and independent adoptions, the cost of adopting an infant in this country has continued to grow, and to an increasing extent, there are concerns that money has come to play too large a role in adoption. At the same time, adoption service providers have proliferated: new adoption agencies have joined traditional agencies, some of which have provided adoption services for decades; a growing number of attorneys specialize in adoption; and in a number of states, facilitators—whose role is to bring together prospective adoptive parents and birth mothers—have begun to add their services to the range of available options.

The market forces affecting infant adoption in the United States today reflect, to a great extent, the dynamics that began in the earlier part of this century. This section traces the history of infant adoption in the U.S. from the perspective of the market issues of money and power. It examines the role that money currently plays in infant adoption, differing perspectives regarding the extent to which money should be a factor in adoption services, and current market responses to the increased cost of infant adoption. It then considers issues of power in infant adoption—power imbalances at the interpersonal level among

3

members of the triad and at the broader societal level and the respective power bases of providers of adoption services.

The Historical Context

The history of infant adoption practice in the United States has been significantly different for Caucasian children and children of color, particularly African American infants. The differing historical contexts have important implications for contemporary and future practice.

The Adoption of Caucasian Infants

The current adoption environment as it relates to Caucasian infants in this country is a reflection of market forces that began to become apparent in the 1920s and evolved into full form in the early 1950s. Although there was a hiatus in the late 1950s and 1960s, when larger numbers of infants were placed for adoption and the competition for infants to adopt was not as fierce as is currently the case [Sorosky et al. 1979]Vthe current environment bears remarkable resemblance to the market conditions typifying adoption from the early 1900s through mid-century. Zelizer [1985, pp. 167–68] notes that in the late 1800s, "there was no market for babies [in the U.S.] . . . yet 50 years later, adoptive parents were eagerly paying $1,000 or more to purchase an infant . . . By the 1950s, a white, healthy infant sold for as much as $10,000." The "startling appreciation in babies' monetary worth" between the mid-19th and mid-20th century was tied to a revolutionary change in societal views of children [Zelizer 1985, p. 168]. In the nineteenth century, children were "taken in" because they would be of economic benefit to families as farm workers or household help. As a result, older children were valued, and babies were essentially "unmarketable" [Zelizer 1985, p. 168]. As the 20th century unfolded, the value of children's labor disappeared and children came to be valued for sentimental reasons, a development which greatly "boosted babies' charm" [Zelizer 1985, p. 168]. The "new emotional worth" of children that came to be recognized in the 1920s and 1930s was shaped by an appeal unconnected to economic value, but nonetheless, children became "increasingly monetized and commercialized" so that "parents were willing to disburse large sums of money to obtain a baby of their own" [Zelizer 1985, p. 171].

A dynamic reminiscent of today's market forces quickly set the stage for a new paradigm for adoption. In the 1920s, *The New York Times* reported a significant change in the forces shaping adoption—the critical problem was "one of finding enough children for childless homes rather than of finding enough homes for homeless children" [cited in Zelizer 1985, p. 190]. The problem persisted, and the ardent search for a child to love through adoption continued into the 1930s and 1940s. During that period, adoption also became "glamorous and romanticized" as a host of famous political figures and Hollywood celebrities openly assumed their positions among the ranks of adoptive parents [Zelizer 1985, p. 190], although, as would later be borne out, sometimes under circumstances strongly suggestive of "baby buying" [Tennessee Black Market Adoption Information 1999]. In some quarters, adoption took on "fairy-tale dimensions" as "poor waifs"— that is, children under the age of three—were portrayed as being transformed almost Cinderella-like through their adoptions by generous and wealthy new parents [Zelizer 1985, pp. 190-191; Tennessee Black Market Adoption Information 1999].

The sentimentally attractive child rather than the economically productive child became valued, and the criteria rendering babies "desirable" became "physical appeal and personality" [Zelizer 1985, p. 193]. The greatest demand was for baby girls, in excellent health and preferably with blue eyes and golden hair [Zelizer 1985]. By the 1920s, methods to test intelligence and determine physical health had been refined and were used to assure adopters that "eugenically speaking," they were not participating "in a grab-bag" [Zelizer 1985, pp. 194-195]. Zelizer [1985, p. 195] states that even stigmas associated with illegitimacy were overcome through representations that "love babies" were of particular desirability and attractiveness.

Baby selling and buying were sufficiently common in the U.S. throughout the first half of the twentieth century to give rise to

federal scrutiny [Zelizer 1985; Tennessee Black Market Adoption
Information 1999]. "Baby selling" was formally declared a national social problem in 1955 when Senator Estes Kefauver con-
vened a Congressional investigation to examine adoption practices across the country. A lucrative black market was
uncovered—notably including the activities of Georgia Tann of
the Tennessee Children's Home Society, who placed over 1,000
children across state lines over a twenty year period, at a profit of
more than a million dollars [Zelizer 1985]. Other activities somewhat less massive in scope also came to light, including those of
Dr. Katherine Cole, a "naturopathic physician" who sold babies in
Miami to adoptive parents from 1927 through the early 1960s
[Cole Babies Website 1999], and the activities of Dr. Thomas J.
Hicks in Georgia, who delivered and sold approximately 200
infants during the 1950s and into the 1960s ["Woman searching"
1997]. The market of the era was fueled by a scarcity of newborns
being placed for adoption and "a growing number of enthusiastic
buyers of healthy white infants" [Zelizer 1985, p. 200]. These
forces, combined with little demand for older children, mirror the
very dynamics that characterize the domestic adoption of infants
today.

The Adoption of African American Infants

The historical patterns generally associated with infant adoption
in the U.S. reflect the course for Caucasian infants but not African
American and other children of color. As Perry [1998, p. 11]
observes, "the history of adoption among Blacks is different from
that of whites." In contrast to general child rearing patterns among
Caucasians, the informal adoption of children has been common
in the African American community. During slavery and after
emancipation, families of slaves or former slaves took in children
orphaned by the death or sale of their parents [Billingsley 1993].
At the same time, the fact that a child was born outside of marriage
did not place social pressures on the mother to make an adoption
plan. African American women had children as a result of rape by
slave owners and other Caucasian males, and these children and

their mothers were not subject to stigmatization as were illegitimate Caucasian children [Perry 1998]. Single mothers were supported by extended family and the community as a whole. As a consequence of these factors, formal adoption was rarely needed or desirable.

At the same time, the formal adoption system historically has not viewed African American women or their children as clients of their services [Perry 1998]. Although societal expectations from the 1930s through the 1960s were that unmarried Caucasian women should place their babies for adoption, African American women were expected to keep their babies and raise them themselves. Solinger [1992] writes that the differential race-based expectations of single mothers flowed from differing societal views of illegitimacy during this era. Illegitimacy among single Caucasian women was associated with psychological problems, whereas illegitimacy among single African American women was viewed as the result of sexual irresponsibility [Solinger 1992]. In the years following World War II, single pregnant African American women became the scapegoats for a host of societal problems, including the growing costs of welfare, the presence of unwanted children in U.S. society, and the endemic poverty among African Americans. In this context, single African American women became the targets of retribution, and "blame"—as opposed to the "shame" typically associated with unwed births by Caucasian women—became the guiding social principle [Solinger 1992]. This punitive dynamic played out with particular force in the context of the Aid to Families with Children enacted in 1935 and implemented in the late 1930s and 1940s. African American women were viewed as foisting a "bad bargain" on society by getting "something"—welfare benefits—for "nothing" and punishment—forcing these women to struggle to raise their children themselves—was deemed appropriate [Solinger 1992, p. 30].

African American women who attempted to subvert societal expectations and place their children for adoption during this era encountered a harsh response. Many of these women were charged with desertion or were otherwise "punished" by being forced to

support their children [Solinger 1992, p. 30]. Extremely few
African American infants were placed for adoption, exceeding no
more than 1.5% of all nonmarital births [Chandra et. al 1999]. The
combined effect of limited interest in formal adoption within the
African American community, race-based social attitudes and
adoption agency practice, and public policy was an extremely low
level of formal adoptions of infants. At the same time, market
forces in the form of high demand for Caucasian infants—but not
African American babies—during this era shaped the nature of
adoption for women and children of color.

The Contemporary Context

The current environment of infant adoption in the United States
is one in which, on the one hand, there has been an increase in the
number of women experiencing infertility [Abma et al. 1997]—a
trend associated with a pattern of delayed child bearing and the
very large cohorts of baby boom women who have moved into
their reproductive years [Abma et al. 1997; Mosher and Pratt
1990]—and, on the other hand, a significant decline in the number
of newborns placed for adoption [Chandra et al. 1999]. As in the
earlier part of the century, the demand for healthy infants significantly exceeds the number of children available for adoption
[Sokoloff 1993]. The 1995 National Survey of Family Growth
found that a growing number of women—500,000 women in the
1995 survey as compared to approximately 200,000 in the 1988
survey—had considered or were considering the adoption of a
child [Chandra et al. 1999]. By contrast—as a result of the legalization of abortion, increased access to contraceptives, and changed
social mores regarding unmarried parenting—the number of Caucasian infants placed for adoption has continued to decline
[Chandra et al. 1999]. As a consequence, the historical gap in
relinquishment rates by unmarried Caucasian and unmarried
African American women has closed [Chandra et al. 1999]. In the
most recent reported time period, 1989-1995, only about 1% of
babies born to never-married women were placed for adoption,
down from 9% before 1973 [Chandra et al. 1999]. The data suggest

a ratio of approximately six adoption seekers for every actual adoption. The marked imbalance between adoption demand and the supply of newborns—of any race—for purposes of adoption has set the stage for a host of market force issues that affect contemporary infant adoption practice.

Money and Infant Adoption: A"Black Market," a "Gray Market," or Simply the "Marketplace"?

Money has become an established feature of infant adoption, a reality that has given rise to a number of questions. Is money merely an aspect of the adoption of newborns as it is with any other service? Or is money playing a negative role, diminishing each member of the triad in different ways? Are, for example, the fees required to adopt an infant taking unfair advantage of prospective adoptive parents? Are the decisions of birth parents unduly influenced by the monetary aspect of adoption? And perhaps most importantly, are infants being transformed into commodities— either because money is involved at any level or because the amount of money associated with their adoptions has escalated so significantly?

Historically, the exchange of money for a child to adopt has been associated with illegal or "black market" activities. The extent to which illegal trafficking in infants has represented the practice of adoption overall at any point in time is not clear [Boskey & Hollinger 1998], but many believe that such activities have tended to be the exception rather than the rule [Duryea 1996]. Periodically, however, revelations of egregious black market activity surface, suggesting a pervasive pattern of illegal practice in certain areas of the country through the 1960s. In a highly publicized recent case in Florida, for example, an adult adoptee in his 40s filed suit to annul his adoption, asserting that a baby broker sold him at the age of eight days to his adoptive parents and that his original birth certificate was deliberately falsified [Moffett 1999]. In the wake of extensive media coverage of the case, it was alleged that thousands of similar black market adoptions were

arranged in Florida from the 1930s through the late 1960s, with
babies brokered at prices ranging from $25 to $3,000 [Moffett
1999].

Though likely to be more characteristic of adoption historically, black market activities are not entirely an artifact of the past.
Black market activities—the outright "child selling" that represents "grotesquely illegal cases" [Duryea 1996, p. 1B]—continue
to capture news headlines, representing the most extreme expression of market force issues in infant adoption practice. Greater
regulation of adoption through state statutes and regulatory agencies, though imperfect in many regards, however, has made it
more difficult for modern day equivalents of Georgia Tann or Dr.
Thomas Hicks to operate extensive baby selling operations. Instead of a broad-based market involving interstate baby selling,
current "black market" activities in this country are generally
conducted by individuals seeking to financially gain through a
single adoptive placement or a limited number of transactions.
One recent case, for example, involved the receipt of broker's fees
by an intermediary operating an illegal adoption agency and
"selling" a teenager's baby for $7,399 [Associated Press 1998].
Other recent exposés have involved birth parents who were
arrested for attempting to sell their children to prospective adoptive parents. In one case, a 21 year old woman was arrested and
charged with fraud for allegedly promising her unborn child to
seven prospective adoptive parents for $16,000 each [Riccardi
1999], and in another case, a Florida couple was arrested and
charged with attempting to sell their twin four-day old boys for
$25,000 [Duryea 1996].

Irrespective of the extent of such activities—or how isolated
such illegal baby or child selling activity by parents or intermediaries may be, they create a disturbing atmosphere surrounding
infant adoption. Although the most egregious efforts may be met
with arrest, fines, or imprisonment for the perpetrators, the fact
that adults are willing to sell children outright for a profit and that
other adults are willing to pay for a child raises concerns about the
insidious effect that money may be playing in infant adoption.

There is broad agreement—legally and ethically—that children may not be "sold" outright for profit, but at what point is the payment of money appropriate in the adoptive placement of a child? Is money an acceptable part of adoption as long as the child is not expressly considered the "product" and a clear profit margin is not generated through the transaction?

Most adoptions of infants in the United States today do not involve the illegal exchange of money but, instead, the payment of fees charged by professionals—usually lawyers or intermediaries such as facilitators—or by adoption agencies. Fee charging in both arenas—independent adoption and agency adoption—has raised a number of issues and brought into question the extent to which money should play a role in the adoption of children, particularly in a highly competitive environment in which supply and demand are significantly out of balance.

There is general agreement that the amount of money involved and the potential for making money in infant adoption has greatly increased since the 1960s. Watson [1999, p. 7] attributes this trend to three key factors: the availability of fewer infants for adoption as a result of legal and social changes; "the growing belief that everything in our country (health, information, peace of mind, children) is a commodity that can be packaged, marketed, and sold at a profit;" and the ability of an increasing number of affluent young adults who are willing to pay whatever is required to satisfy their desire to become parents. These factors suggest that the escalation in the amount of money involved in infant adoption is the result of the combined effects of diminished supply, an adult sense of entitlement, and affluence. This combination of factors provides the environment in which independent and agency adoptions take place.

Independent Adoptions

In the arena of independently arranged adoptions of infants, the charging of fees is a broadly accepted practice. It is legal in most states for attorneys to broker arrangements between birth and adoptive parents and charge fees for their services, and it is legal for adoptive parents to pay birth parents' expenses for medical care and in some cases, living and travel expenses during pregnancy [Bosky & Hollinger 1998]. These laws, however, vary significantly from one state to another. Some states specifically define the expenses that may be paid [see Vermont Statutes 1999]; others broadly refer to "reasonable and necessary expenses" [see Arizona Revised Statutes Annotated 1999]; and yet others are known for their very permissive rules. One such permissive state is Louisiana, where according to one writer, "laws are lax, where the business is unregulated, and where adoption lawyers from across the country often come to nest" [Escobar 1998, p. C1].

Independent adoptions currently range in cost from $8,000 to $30,000 [Jacoby 1999]. Dramatically larger figures are, at times, reported in connection with independent adoption, with reports that a few prospective adoptive parents have paid as much as $100,000 in order to adopt a newborn [Mansnerus 1998]. Irrespective of how the law of any state may define what constitutes appropriate fees and costs in connection with an adoption, expenses charged to adoptive parents are largely unregulated. Although courts are required under most state laws to review the fees and expenses associated with any adoption, the amounts are rarely questioned by judges who do not closely scrutinize such reports [Watson 1999; Escobar 1998]. In addition, a successful outcome for the "paying customers"—that is, adoptive parents who have a baby placed with them—may create a situation in which those who are charged significant amounts are unlikely to lodge a complaint against their attorney for excessive fees. Some note that in the name of the "noble end" of adoption, the parties may be willing to tolerate "some shenanigans" [Escobar 1998, p. C01].

Those critical of independent adoption have referred to it as a "gray market" [Duryea 1996, p. 1B] or as a "modified legitimate market" [Zelizer 1985, p. 204]. Implicit in these characterizations is an assumption that lawyers and other professionals involved in infant adoption do not seek to profit directly from the transaction—as would be the case in "black market" activities—but do realize substantial fees for services rendered. The concern appears to arise, in part, from the very ambiguity that characterizes the charges involved in such adoptions. Duryea [1996] describes independent adoptions as "danc[ing] the line between legal and illegal," and Zelizer [1985, p. 204] notes that the "boundary between a legitimate market and a 'dangerous' sale is not always easy to maintain." Wright [cited in Mansnerus 1998, p. A16] observes that there is now only the thinnest line between "buying a child" and "buying adoption services that lead to a child." The ambiguity is heightened by other factors: the "considerable uncertainty. . . as to what constitutes an unlawful payment" and the generally weak sanctions when a payment is obviously improper [Boskey & Hollinger 1998, pp. 3-29].

Though some have maintained that the "alleged perils" associated with independent adoptions of infants may be overstated [see Boskey & Hollinger 1998], there are a number of questions that arise in relation to this practice. To what extent do the fiscal realities surrounding independent adoptions—both in terms of the fees charged by the professional and the expenses that are paid to the birth mother—create an environment in which money has come to play an overarching role? Are adoptive parents—placed in a situation in which they are paying significant amounts of money—entitled, as a result, to a baby? Does the ambiguity surrounding birth parent "expenses" create an environment in which either birth parents' "needs" are inflated or birth mothers develop a sense of obligation to the adoptive parents to follow through on adoptions? And at what point do the fees charged in an independent adoption become such that it is an infant—and not the professional's "services"—that is being purchased?

Agency Adoptions

Similar issues may be raised with regard to agency-arranged adoptions, as virtually all agencies that place infants and very young children for adoption also charge fees. Until the 1940s, agencies only accepted donations from adoptive parents who, out of a sense of gratitude, wished to contribute financially to their agencies [Zelizer 1985]. The introduction of adoption fees in the 1940s was not without controversy and raised ethical and profes-

sional concerns for some. Zelizer [1985, p. 201] observes that
when agencies made the decision to charge fees:

> An apparently profound contradiction was thereby cre-
> ated, between a cultural system that declared children
> priceless emotional assets, and a social arrangement that
> treated them as 'cash commodities.'

Agencies—which by and large were not-for-profit entities—
justified the charging of fees on several bases. First, many agencies
pointed out that they limited fees to actual costs, a position that
most agencies continue to take with regard to the fees they charge
today. Other agencies pointed to their practices of charging only
nominal fees or utilizing a sliding fee scale based on prospective
adoptive parents' ability to pay, practices that to some degree are
utilized by adoption agencies currently but more typically in
relation to "special needs," not infant, adoption. Zelizer [1985, p.
205] notes that agencies also legitimized fees as "a symbolic
payment" that assisted adoptive parents to meet their desire to
financially support the agency by providing them with specific
guidelines rather than expecting them to rely on an ill-defined and
possibly inadequate standard of "gratitude." By the 1970s, the
broader social environment had begun to define infant adoption
services in consumer-oriented, as opposed to social service, terms.
Davis [2000] notes that during this period, the United Way, for
example, discontinued its giving to nonprofit agencies for their
infant adoption programs. The rationale for this decision was that
prospective adoptive parents were the primary clients of these
services; their incomes exceeded the income level of clients
typically served by nonprofit organizations; and consequently,
prospective adoptive parents could cover the cost of services
through the payment of fees [Davis 2000].

Estimates vary as to the current level of agency fees that
typically are charged. The low end of the fee range for domestic
adoptions of infants is estimated at $4,000 by one source [Jacoby
1999] and as high as $15,000 by another [Pertman 1998]. Both of
these sources set the upper end of the fee range at about $30,000
[Jacoby 1999; Pertman 1998]. As with independent adoptions—
where the fee structure is not considerably different from the

upper end of agency fees—fee-charging by adoption agencies raises questions about the extent to which money, even in the not-for-profit arena, has assumed a role in adoption practice. In the context of agency-arranged adoptions, an examination of money in relation to infant adoption raises both philosophical issues about whether money in the form of fees should be involved at all and questions about the amount of money that can be justified as appropriate in this service arena. Are fees for adoption appropriate? And, if they can be justified, what constitutes an "appropriate" level of fee?

Adoption Fees: Justifiable or Unjustified?

Whether the issue of fees paid by prospective adoptive parents arises in the context of agency or independent adoption, there are very different views of whether fees are inherently proper in light of what adoption fees purchase. One school of thought vigorously supports the propriety of fee charging, although justifications vary. Even among those who most avidly advocate professional fees, however, profit making is rarely, if ever, utilized as the justification. Zelizer [1985, p. 207] notes that "even market ideologists and practitioners ultimately justify baby selling by criteria other than profit. Payments are legitimized as symbolic expressions of sentimental concern." Exemplifying the sentimental justification is the argument that the payment of large fees is of psychological benefit and reassurance to the adoptee. One attorney known for his work in arranging independent adoptions, for example, argues:

> How would I feel if my father paid ten thousand dollars to adopt me? Boy, that guy really wanted me . . . He paid that much for me, he really wanted me that much . . . What could be a greater sense of self than that somebody sacrificed so much to have me? . . . [McTaggart 1980, p. 318, quoting Stanley Michelman].

Child welfare professionals may be skeptical of this rationale for the charging of large fees, particularly as it seems to suggest that the higher the fee the better, an outcome of none-too-incidental benefit to the very adoption professionals who advance this line of reasoning. Gritter [1999, p. 11] may articulate a more persuasive viewpoint on this issue: "For the child, there is no consolation for the thought that one has been sold and purchased."

Others justify fees on pure economic grounds. Landes and Posner [1978, p. 341], for example, argue that the market best resolves issues that arise in infant adoption. They contend that "the baby shortage and black market are the result of legal restrictions that prevent the market from operating freely in the sale of babies as of other goods. This suggests as a possible reform simply eliminating these restrictions" [Landes & Posner 1978, p. 341]. Dismissing the moral outrage against the "sale of babies" as outdated and impractical, they argue that through an undiluted pricing system, there would be more efficiency in matching children and adoptive parents, and adoption, as an institution, would consequently benefit. In a subsequent book, Posner [1992], in fact, explained that if a law of supply and demand ruled, there would be a decrease in the cost of adoption so that adopting a baby would cost no more than a car. William Pierce, former president of the National Council for Adoption, elaborating on that theme, agrees:

> This is a capitalist system where the laws of the market work their magic. People don't seem to believe that $16,000 or $17,000 is too much for a new car. If we're going to have a quality service, you're going to have to pay for it [Pertman 1998, p. A11].

Gritter [1999, p. 10] notes that the market pricing viewpoint of those like Landes and Posner is based on an assumption that "the unencumbered natural laws of economics will appropriately govern the process" of adoption and that "the fewer the regulations, the better."

Boskey and Hollinger [1998, pp. 3-28], however, note that "few have taken [these] suggestions seriously." They contend that neither a contractual nor a market model has been accepted as a basis for the adoptive placement of infants and that, instead, "donative transfer" has been the prevailing concept underlying infant adoption. Although "donative" intent may stand as the theoretical basis for infant adoption and may have greater appeal than a pure market analysis, it presents difficulties in actual application given the escalating sums of money involved in the adoption of very young children. In the strictest sense of "donation," money would play no or, at most, a nominal role.

In direct contrast to the position of Landes and Posner is Watson's view that fees charged prospective adoptive parents are not appropriate under any circumstances [1999]. This position has not been advocated by attorneys practicing in the field of adoption—where adoption services may be viewed as no different than any other matter for which the attorney charges a fee—but it has been raised in relation to agency-arranged adoptions. Watson is clear that he believes that the exchange of money in independently arranged adoptions is improper, but he targets his concerns principally on fee-charging by agencies, which he believes is an unjustified process. While recognizing that the potential for financial exploitation is particularly great in independent adoption, he contends that the possibility of financial exploitation exists in agency adoptions, though perhaps in a more subtle form [1999]. He views agencies as, by and large, reflecting good social work practice, but he takes issue with most agencies' reliance, at least in part, on fees charged to adoptive parents. He questions the justification that fees cover the costs of services and do not involve a payment for a child. Specifically, he points to the widely varying definitions of what constitutes "services to adoptive parents" and maintains that this variation "is based less on the quality of agency service than on the fiscal base of an agency and how it calculates its fees" [1999, p. 7].

In line with Watson's vigorous attack on adoption fees are those who argue that adoption fees are essentially the equivalent of "child buying" and that adoptive parents are aware of this reality. In a 1975 hearing before the Congressional Subcommittee on Children and Youth, for example, the director of an organization of adopted adults testified that:

> It . . . doesn't matter to the people involved . . . whether the fee was $5,000 or $25,000 and whether it was paid to an agency or to an independent agent . . . No rationale of

fees will relieve adoptive parents of the certain knowledge that they have bought a human being [Hearings
Before the Subcommittee on Children and Youth 1975,
pg. 76].

Gritter likewise notes that adoptive parents cannot help but
be on notice of the nature of the transaction. He writes that "when
adoptive parents pay $25,000 for 10 hours of service, it is difficult
to pretend that they are paying for services rendered . . . They are
buying a product" [1999, p. 11]. Watson similarly argues that
"whatever the agency charges, adoptive parents are not deceived.
They know they are paying for a child" [1999, p. 7]. He takes the
position that "any fee paid to anyone in any adoption is exploitative and inappropriate" and that "adoptions must be financed
either by tax dollars or by voluntary contributions—but never
contributions from people who are seeking adoption services or
receiving them" [1999, p. 8].

Irrespective of the position taken with regard to the propriety
of charging fees, there is agreement that at least some costs
associated with adoption represent actual expenses connected
with the provision of services and must be met in some way. It is
difficult to ignore the business realities that have prompted and
sustained the practice of charging fees. In independently arranged
adoptions, lawyers provide time and expertise, as do professionals in adoption agencies. Fees also include actual costs related to
travel, the development and assembling of required documenta-
tion, and other expenses specific to the adoption being arranged.
In addition, agencies incur expenses in the operation of their
overall adoption service program. Agencies counsel many women
who ultimately make the decision to raise their children themselves rather than place their children for adoption. One estimate
is that currently 80% of women who work with licensed agencies
make the decision to parent their children [Mansnerus 1998]. This
outcome is broadly supported by child welfare professionals who
view counseling of birth parents as a process that empowers them
to make the best decision for themselves and their children [Child
Welfare League of America 2000]. From an economic perspective,
however, fees charged to adoptive parents who adopt the children

of the 20% of birth mothers who decide in favor of adoption play a critical role for agencies, defraying some portion of the costs of serving the substantial number of birth parents who do not place their children for adoption [Mansnerus 1998].

Little has been published delineating the specific items that comprise the cost of the adoption of an infant in the United States. Pertman [1998], however, has estimated that, on average, an adoption fee of an estimated $24,000 is comprised of the costs of providing the birth mother with health care and counseling (25%); expenses associated with locating the birth father (6%); home studies (10%); travel and living expenses in another state or county (8%); attorney and other legal fees (8%); advertising and other marketing to find birth parents who might place their children for adoption (13%); fees that support subsidies for adoptive parents with lower incomes or who adopt children with special needs (13%); and administrative overhead and salaries (17%). His analysis suggests legitimate expenses associated with the provision of adoption services with no specific item—either in terms of actual expenses incurred or professional services rendered—playing an excessive role in the overall fee structure.

Questions, however, might arise about the assessment of fees to individual adoptive parents for the "services" they are receiving—particularly those expenses assessed to adoptive parents that are unconnected with the individual's own adoption plan. Should, for example, adoptive parents contribute to an agency's advertising and marketing directed to birth parents? To what extent is it appropriate for one adoptive parent to subsidize the costs associated with adoptions by other parents? Does the fact that an adoption fee incorporate such expenses make the case for Watson's contention that the costs associated with adoption should be borne by the community rather than adoptive parents? Or alternatively, is it appropriate that adoptive parents pay not only for their own services but share in other costs incurred by the service provider, as is the case in other service environments? Do the answers to these questions rest on who is considered the "client" in adoption services—the adoptive parent or the child?

Market Responses to the Increased Cost of Infant Adoption

The current market environment of infant adoption—in which the cost of adoption is substantial and shows no indication of stabilizing—has not precipitated any significant effort to set limits on the amount of money involved. Instead, at both the market level—through adoption cancellation insurance—and the policy level—through tax credits—the response has focused on strategies to underwrite the escalating costs of adoption rather than controlling them.

The development of "adoption cancellation" insurance signals a market response to the growing financial burden imposed on prospective adoptive parents. In cases in which prospective adoptive parents pay some or all of the birth mother's medical and living expenses during pregnancy and the birth mother decides not to place her child for adoption, adoption cancellation insurance reimburses the adoptive parents for certain out-of-pocket expenses. First offered nationally in 1993, these policies—by reimbursing expenses incurred for adoptions arranged directly through pre-approved adoption agencies and lawyers [Ramsey 1999]—seek to protect prospective adoptive parents from financial losses when the investment they have made does not yield the anticipated benefit of a baby. The availability of this type of insurance further highlights the growing commercial environment in which adoption is taking place and raises several issues for consideration. Is the availability of insurance against financial "losses" in adoption a smart approach to limiting the financial impact on prospective adoptive parents when an adoption does not take place? Is it simply a response to other market forces in adoption? Alternatively, does such insurance contribute to the commercialization of infant adoption by underwriting the increasing expenses involved and treating an unsuccessful attempt to adopt as an insurable loss?

Like adoption cancellation insurance, federal policy has acknowledged the increasing role of money in infant adoption and the escalating costs associated with adopting a young child. Rather than attempting to exert control over or oversight of the cost of adoption, federal policy has tended to favor tax-based subsidies to assist adopters meet the increasing costs of adoption. Under current law (as of early 2000), adoptive families with incomes of $75,000 or less may receive a full tax credit up to $5,000 for expenses incurred in adopting a child, a credit that phases out as income increases and is eliminated at an income level of $115,000.

Recent legislative efforts have focused on increasing the tax credit to $10,000 and raising the income limit to $150,000, signaling an interest in assisting higher income families defray a greater portion of the increasing costs associated with infant (and international) adoption. The proposed doubling of the tax credit suggests a recognition that costs have continued to grow, but it is not clear what role tax credits may be playing in fueling additional increases in adoption fees. Has, for example, the tax credit at the current level simply served to increase the cost of an adoption by an equivalent amount? The rising cost of adoption may be associated, at least to some degree, with the availability of such subsidies. At the same time, the proposed increase in income eligibility for the tax credit suggests an interest in supporting adoptions by higher-income families—families who are able to meet the current high level of fees at the outset and who may have chosen to adopt even in the absence of a tax credit. As a consequence, the question may focus on the most appropriate allocation of resources if the goal is to encourage adoption. The structure of the tax credit does not benefit families who adopt children in foster care—typically families of moderate means who incur few up front costs in adopting but who may be in greater need of ongoing financial supports to meet the special needs of the children they adopt, an issue discussed later in this volume.

Money and Infant Adoption: The Impact on Triad Members

The increasing role of money in infant adoption gives rise to a host of ethical considerations affecting prospective adoptive parents, birth parents, and children. The issues vary for each triad member.

It may be that the increased costs associated with adopting infants in this country most directly impact prospective adoptive parents who are the parties required to finance adoption services. With regard to the impact of money on these individuals, how should the costs of adoption be viewed? Are prospective adoptive parents being victimized by the process or are they willing participants? One view is that prospective adoptive parents are being exploited by the increasing fees they are required to pay in order to adopt. Having struggled with infertility, they may be willing to pay any level of fee that is charged because they are desperate to be parents. Another perspective is that prospective adoptive parents have created the environment in which higher fees can be charged. Adoptive parents may be willing to pay a fee at any level if it means that they can adopt a baby who meets their age, race, or health preferences. The individuals who adopt infants in this country are, by and large, relatively affluent, and the level of fees that are charged tend to be within their means. A third perspective is that, although the current structure effectively "prices out" individuals of more modest means, the supply of infants is so limited in relation to the demand that higher fees effectively constrain the growth in the number of prospective adopters. Affluence, thus, serves as a mechanism for limiting the pool of adoption seekers. It also enhances the financial opportunities of those who provide adoption services.

From an ethical perspective, important questions are raised by each of these views of the forces shaping the marketplace and their impact on prospective adoptive parents:

- Are adoption professionals—in general, within certain professional groups, or as individuals—taking advantage of the desperation of infertile individuals who turn to adoption? Are high fees representative of simply what professionals judge that the market will bear?

- Are prospective adoptive parents so intent on achieving parenthood through adoption that they have, in effect, pushed the fees upward through a willingness to pay more to ensure the desired outcome for themselves?

- Has the increasing role of money created an environment in which only the affluent can afford to adopt—thereby attaining a privileged status denied to those of more modest means? Is the opportunity to parent a young healthy child through adoption increasingly becoming reserved for a financial elite?

Equally troubling is the extent to which the increasing sums of money associated with the adoption of infants may impact birth parents, particularly their decision-making regarding adoption. The relationship between adoptive parents and birth parents may be skewed when money is involved. Gritter [1999, p. 11] notes:

When a prospective adoptive family 'invests' in a prospective birth parent, they expect a return on their investment. . . In complementary fashion, birth parents can easily feel indebted and trapped by their financial dependence on the prospective adoptive parents. The financial support may add to their reluctance to change their course, even if they feel that the right thing is to set aside the adoption intentions. Predictably, the cessation of support when the adoptive arrangements are complete can also add to the birth parent's feeling of being used and dropped. Another worrisome possibility is that expectant birth parents may exploit the desperation of prospective adoptive parents by misleading them about their intentions.

Because the emotional context of adoption may "add enormously to the vulnerability of the participants" [Gritter 1999, p. 11], there are important issues related to the potential impact that large sums of money may have on birth parents, particularly when the relationship is arranged directly by the parties. From an ethical perspective, these questions may include:

- To what extent do prospective adoptive parents' expenditures to cover a birth mother's medical costs or other living expenses create a sense of indebtedness that may affect her decision-making? To what extent might the interpersonal relationship that surrounds the financial support unduly influence her decision-making? Does a birth mother ultimately "owe" it to the prospective adoptive parents to follow-through on the adoption because a good deal of money has been expended on her behalf?

- Alternatively, to what extent does the prospect of obtaining a large sum of money in connection with adoption attract the unscrupulous—individuals who, assessing the lucrative market, fabricate pregnancies and/or intentions to place their children for adoption or precipitate "bidding wars" as they play one prospective adoptive parent against another?

A new and perplexing issue related to the potential impact of money on birth parents is raised by legislation recently introduced in Kansas, which would provide women who place their children for adoption—but not women who choose to raise their children themselves—with a $5,000 tax credit [Stanfield 2000; Kansas Legislative Services 2000]. Its sponsor offered a two-pronged rationale for this type of tax credit: to reduce the number of abortions in the state by assisting women to pay for personal and medical expenses during pregnancy and to encourage adoption, contending that "if they [birth mothers] are doing something the state wants them to do, then the state should help" [Stanfield 2000, citing Rep. Thomas Klein, p. 2].

Objections to this legislative proposal have taken several forms. Some have argued that the tax credit is objectionable on the grounds that it is, in essence, the equivalent to the purchase of a baby. One legislator, for example, stated, "We don't want women providing children for $5,000 a pop. We don't want it to be a market" [Stanfield 2000, citing Rep. Billie Vining, p. 2]. Other issues relate to the sponsor's stated rationales for the tax credit approach. If reduction in abortion rates is indeed the policy goal, the tax credit should be available for women who choose to parent their children as well as for women who place their children for adoption. The fact that the tax credit does not benefit parenting women suggests that the goal may be, in reality, to free more infants for adoption. With regard to the assertion that the "state" wants women to place their children for adoption, serious questions are raised regarding whether such a goal is desirable public policy and to what extent the state should facilitate that outcome through financial incentives [Stanfield 2000]. Should relinquishment be promoted? Is the encouragement of relinquishment, in reality, an effort to expand the supply of infants available for adoption? Is money—in the form of a tax credit—being used to induce a decision by women whose economic circumstances may make them particularly vulnerable?

Finally, there are the critical ethical issues surrounding the impact on children of the increasing role of money in adoption. In essence, the question has become whether infants have been transformed into commodities, rated on the basis of age, race, gender, health, physical attractiveness, or other desired characteristics, and available to those individuals who are able to pay the highest fee. Are infants simply another product that may be purchased by those who are able and willing to pay the most money? Has money essentially changed the face of infant adoption from a service for children to a service for affluent adults?

As these questions suggest, the issues related to the role of money in infant adoption are significant, and they are not likely to abate. Mansnerus [1998, p. A1] writes that with the increasing imbalance between the supply of "white American born infants" and the demand by "unhappily infertile couples"—trends showing no indication of slowing in the future [Freundlich 1998]—money has come to "play a defining role in determining who will succeed in this desperate quest for that which cannot be legally bought or sold." Quoting Graham Wright, president of the California Association of Adoption Agencies, she writes [1998, p. A1], "If you have enough money, you'll get what you think you want."

Power and the Adoption of Infants

Connected with, but somewhat distinct from, issues related to the role of money in infant adoption are issues of power. Questions about the extent to which the parties to adoption hold and exercise power arise in three key contexts: first, in the interpersonal realm which reflects the different levels of power held by prospective adoptive parents and by birth parents; second, in the social, political, and economic realms in which power in adoption is intertwined with issues of race, culture, class, and gender; and third, in the realm of the marketplace itself in which competing players may vie for the infant adoption "business."

The Power Held by Prospective Adoptive Parents and by Birth Parents

At the interpersonal level of infant adoption is the relationship between adoptive parents and birth parents at the time that the decision to place a child for adoption is made. What power is held by prospective adoptive parents and by birth parents? How does power affect the way in which infant adoption takes place? Some argue that power has come to characterize infant adoption largely because of commercialization. Gritter [1999] notes that in a "business" environment, certain dynamics shape the nature of the services provided—and priority is typically placed on the needs and interests of the "paying customer." When adoption is treated as a "business," with attention on the "paying customer," Gritter [1999, p. 9] maintains that "the unmistakable motivation . . . is to satisfy the desires of infertile families." Prospective adoptive parents hold power that flows from material advantage in an environment in which the other members of the triad are likely to have limited (as in the case of birth parents) or no (as in the case of children) economic resources. As a consequence, from the perspective of the adoption professional or adoption agency, it is the prospective adoptive parent who is likely to be the primary, if not exclusive, "client" because he or she pays the fee for the services.

Quite apart from a definition of power based on ability to pay is power based on social stature. In this context, the adoptive parent also is likely to hold greater power than is the birth parent. Gritter [1999, p. 11], addressing this perspective, writes that control essentially rests with adoptive parents who may "lack the power to overcome the quirks and vagaries of biology," but who interpersonally "remain resourceful and potent," not only financially but because of superior educational and social advantages over birth parents. Social acceptance, if not admiration, further enhances the position of adoptive parents. Research suggests that the general public is likely to perceive adoptive parents in more highly positive ways than they are likely to view birth parents [The Evan B. Donaldson Adoption Institute 1997].

The power inequities inherent in infant adoption do not necessarily manifest themselves in each adoption. Gritter [1999, p. 9] notes that "the basic decency of prospective adoptive parents usually calms [the] uncomfortable contrast" between adoptive parents and birth parents. What manifests on a general basis, however, is "a system that is tilted toward adoptive parents," a situation that is "not likely to produce balanced adoptive relationships" between adoptive and birth parents [Gritter 1999, p. 9]. Because they control the availability of the "desired commodity," the argument is sometimes made that birth parents hold power over prospective adoptive parents [Davis 2000]. Likewise, it is often contended that the power of birth parents has grown over the past several years as they have gained opportunities to personally select adoptive families for their children [Romanchik 1996]. The reality remains, however, that birth parents generally do not feel empowered in the adoption process and that adoptive parents, because they usually bring greater social and financial advantages compared to those of most birth parents, hold greater power with adoption service providers [Romanchik 1996]. These inequities raise important issues in the context of the "marketplace" and how services are provided.

Power and Its Relationship to Race, Color, Class, and Gender

Undergirding the power inequities that may characterize the interpersonal relationships between adoptive and birth parents are broader socioeconomic and socio-cultural considerations.

Wegar [1997, p. 36] writes that "race and class, along with gender, age, family structure, and sexual preference, are major structuring principles in the American adoption system," suggesting that there are distinct sociocultural and economic factors characterizing those who adopt and those whose children historically have been adopted.

Race and class have played particularly powerful roles in relation to the children who are placed for adoption and the prospective adoptive parents who are provided the opportunity to adopt [Howe 1995, 1997; Perry 1998]. Race, in particular, has been a significant factor in the determination of which infants are adoption-desirable and which prospective adoptive parents are likely to be served. Historically, Caucasian infants have held preferred status in adoption services [Perry 1998]. Because of the significant decrease in the number of healthy Caucasian infants available for adoption, however, desirability in terms of the racial backgrounds of infants to be placed for adoption has been redefined, and there is now greater demand for infants of color. At the same time, the number of Caucasian adults seeking to adopt has continued to rise [Chandra et al. 1999]. The increased demand among Caucasians for infants to adopt is likely to have implications for the level of adoption services provided Caucasian adopters—which historically has been high—and families of color— which historically has been quite low. Howe [1995, 1997] argues that supply and demand dynamics have created a market in which economic and political forces related to race predominate.

Drawing on the work of demographer Gabrielle Sandor [1994], Howe [1995, p. 147] suggests that with the decline in the availability of Caucasian infants available for adoption, the increasing incidence of biracial births in this country constitutes a "growing potential new source of infants." The increase in biracial births, though clearly evident from small data samples, has been difficult to fully quantify on a nationwide basis as a result of the racial categories used in census reporting prior to the year 2000 [Sandor 1994; Schemo 2000]. Even in the absence of definitive census data, however, data clearly indicate increasing rates of interracial marriage rates [Lind 1998] and with that trend, higher rates of mixed-race births [Sandor 1994]. Howe [1995, p. 148] writes that a further implication of these trends toward higher rates of interracial marriage and marital mixed-race births is greater interracial cohabitation and nonmarital biracial births. She concludes "it is reasonable to infer that many of these babies . . . might be relinquished for adoption" [1995, p. 148]. In her view, the greater desirability of these infants—as Caucasian prospective adopters find that the shrinking supply of Caucasian infants presents formidable barriers to adoption—has triggered policy and practice changes to enhance the access of Caucasians to infants of color [Howe 1995]. She argues, for example, that federal policy changes that prohibit any consideration of race in adoptive placements are designed to enhance the access of prospective Caucasian adoptive parents to a new supply of infants [Howe 1995]. She writes that prohibitions against considering race in placing infants with adoptive families are:

> . . . a maneuver to enable whites who seek to adopt infants to gain access to the growing number of nonmarital, mixed-race children who may be relinquished for adoption, free of the constraints imposed by same-race or same-culture placement preferences. . . Considering the fact that "African American families throughout the country are waiting to adopt infants and that African American families adopt at a rate of 4.5 times greater than European-American or Hispanic families" [citing McKenzie 1993, p. 72], this trend could be characterized as an attempt to garner the market in infants [1995, p. 149].

Perry [1998, p. 153] agrees with this assessment, noting:

> Since whites in this society are generally more affluent than Blacks, in a price war, white families would generally be in a position to outbid Black families for children of color. Since it is newborns who are most desired for adoption, regardless of race, the market approach could

enable white families to corner the market on all babies, including healthy newborns of color. This would virtually shut out Black families from having the chance to adopt these children.

These writers highlight the combined effect of race and socioeconomic status on promoting the position of Caucasian adopters—to the detriment of African American adopters—in a market in which children of color have become increasingly desirable.

Mandell [1973], in an earlier commentary, similarly contended that adoption has been based on and has reinforced class inequities in which the affluent, as a group, historically have dominated the poor and the socially stigmatized. She [1973, p. 29] writes:

To obtain children, the middle and upper classes are more likely than the working and lower classes to turn to adoption agencies rather than to relatives and informal community contacts. The adopted children come not only from strangers, but frequently from poor strangers and from unmarried mothers, who have a stigmatized social status.

Benet [1976, p. 70] likewise has referred to the power of "the white ruling group" in socioeconomic terms, but with a primary focus on the ability of those in power to regulate the reproductive behavior of poor women. Research suggests, in line with her concerns about the powerlessness of women with limited resources, that many women who place their infants for adoption in the United States do so because they cannot afford to raise their children themselves [Edwards 1999]. Perry [1998, p. 101] has observed that this dynamic is particularly troubling in the context of the transracial adoptions of African American children, noting that these adoptions "often result in the transfer of children from the least advantaged women to the most advantaged."

It is also the case, however, that historically, many women who placed their children for adoption, particularly in the 1950s and 1960s, were white and of middle class backgrounds and made adoption plans not because of poverty but because of social pressures [Edwards 1999]. In this connection, some feminists attribute to adoption the norms and power allocation of a male-dominated society and view adoption as having punitive effects on the lives of unmarried women who "have violated patriarchal ideals of family life" [Wegar 1997, p. 37]. Perry [1998, p. 137] argues that marital status and financial resources continue to be relevant to mothers' decisions to make adoption plans and reflect the ongoing patriarchal nature of this society:

> As a general matter, unmarried women are economically less well off than married women, and single mothers are disproportionately poor. The poor economic status of women who are not attached to men as financial providers is a reflection of a patriarchal system that still denies to women the same opportunities it accords to men. . . The stigma (of bearing a child outside of marriage) too is largely a function of patriarchy in its quest to control the sexuality and reproductive powers of women.

Although power related to gender and marital status, particularly in relation to the stigma of unwed pregnancy, may have been greater through the 1970s than at present, economic pressures and, for some women, social stigmatization continue to account for placements of infants for adoption today [Edwards 1999; Perry 1998]. The full range of sociocultural factors related to power inequities in adoption—poverty, social stigma, and gender—may apply with particular relevance to contemporary international adoption practice, an issue discussed later in this book.

Power in the Marketplace

The third arena in which issues of power play out is in the marketplace of infant adoption itself. Power in relation to market position may have taken on new meaning with the "surge of entrepreneurial interest in adoption" as new agencies, attorneys and facilitators "hang out their shingles daily" [Pertman 1998, p. A11]. In an increasingly competitive environment for the infant adoption "business," new practices have evolved as providers of adoption services attempt to gain power and obtain a competitive edge. Gritter [1999, p. 10] maintains that the commercial environment of adoption has become "unabashedly competitive," characterized by an "every-man-for-himself" attitude, and those providing adoption services increasingly find that their market toehold can be sustained only if healthy infants can be speedily provided.

As lawyers and other adoption service providers strive to meet the demands of the marketplace, they have developed cutting edge techniques to enhance their market position. Some note that lawyers, in fact, have replaced social workers as the "key players" in adoption [Howe 1995, pp. 148-149], and as such, are particularly active in cultivating new clients. Advertising and new marketing strategies are increasingly used to attract paying customers, an issue discussed later in this volume. Other creative recruitment strategies are used to enhance the probability of making a successful and expeditious adoptive placement. In California, for example, described by Mansnerus [1998] as "the most hospitable to the new entrepreneurialism," adoption lawyers and facilitators now may actively recruit birth mothers on behalf of the prospective adoptive parents they represent. Individuals, identifying themselves as "adoption consultants," are able to create and franchise adoption "agencies," which work principally with lawyers in private practice to facilitate infant adoptions [Howe 1995, p. 151 n.111].

In other areas of the country, minimal oversight of infant adoption maximizes financial opportunities. In Louisiana, for example, the adoption code is widely seen as having "enough gray to overwhelm back and white" [Escobar 1998, p. CO1]. According to some observers, baby brokers utilize legal loopholes to bring pregnant women into the state from other states and other countries, support birth mothers through very broadly defined "reasonable expenses," and charge prospective adoptive parents a host of fees, including charges to find " a suitable birth mother" [Escobar 1998, p. C01; DeFede 1999/2000].

The market has also witnessed the entry of entirely new players, including a burgeoning cast of consultants specializing in services to help prospective adoptive parents to market themselves to prospective birth mothers [Mansnerus 1998]. These practices, discussed more fully later, raise a number of questions, including the extent to which "adoption consultants" are parlaying their services into yet another competitive business component in the infant adoption arena.

In addition to the entry of a host of individual entrepreneurs into the infant adoption marketplace, there has been rapid growth in the number of licensed adoption agencies over the past several years [Mansnerus 1998]. As with the increasingly competitive activities of lawyers, adoption agency practices have been subject to criticism as agencies have attempted to sustain their power base. Howard [1984, p. 510] writes, with regard to both public and private adoption agencies, that their power "in its least defensible aspect" reflects "a purely self-centered institutional interest in continuing to play the role of a power-broker within the child welfare system." She [1984, p. 528] sees agencies' opposition to independent adoption as evidence of their preoccupation with power and interprets this position as a "reflection of such empire-building." Though her interpretation may correctly identify some of the power dynamics among adoption agencies, it may overlook other factors, including professional social work concerns about the nature and scope of counseling and preparation provided by independent practitioners to both birth and adoptive parents. Nonetheless, it has become clear that at least some of the new agencies entering the field of infant adoption do so in the belief that infant adoption services will generate money for their agencies. How should their entry into the field and their commercial motivation be viewed? Is the desire to make money inappropriate in light of the service being provided, essentially irrelevant, or mistaken in light of the saturation of the market by the current cadre of independent practitioners and agencies?

The expansion of the infant adoption marketplace in terms of the number of service providers and the increasing competition among those providers have led some commentators to urge greater regulation of adoption. Hogan [1999a, p. 1], for example, argues that regulation of infant adoption at the state level has been so lax that it has left "consumers of adoption services . . . almost entirely vulnerable to unscrupulous providers effectively shielded by distant geography from accountability." State laws generally require that agencies and individuals who place children for adoption meet licensing requirements, but some experts note that licensing laws tend to be poorly enforced [Terpstra 2000]. Hogan [1999a] maintains that the laxity of regulation means that "adoption effectively remains the only unregulated business in the United States," although other experts point to other child welfare services that receive equally poor oversight [Terpstra 2000]. Federal oversight of domestic adoption has been suggested [Hogan 1999a], but the realities associated with the U.S. system of federalism—in which states regulate family law matters, including adoption—makes this attractive solution unlikely.

Summary

The adoption of infants in the U.S. is characterized by market forces involving money and power. Money has come to play a powerful role in the adoption of very young children, and competition among adoption service providers has become more intense. The largely unregulated environment has given rise to a host of ethical questions related to the impact of market forces on children, birth parents, and prospective adoptive parents, as well as on the institution of adoption itself.

To what extent has infant adoption become a "business"? And to the extent that business considerations characterize infant adoption, is this reality "good" or "bad"? Gritter notes that:

> [t]he institution is swiftly shifting from a professional model, in which service providers hang their shingles and aspire to suspended self-interests, to a business model that aggressively recruits consumers on a buyer-beware basis. An age of commercialism is upon us.

Notwithstanding any advantages that the business world may bring to adoption, Gritter maintains that "adoption is not meant to be a business" [1999, p. 9]. If infant adoption has become "a no-nonsense business transaction" as Gritter suggests [1999, p. 9], it may well have lost the aspirations that defined it as a service for children. On the other hand, the "business" aspects of infant adoption might be viewed simply as legitimate components of operating a service program, and the argument could be made that business viability concerns and aspirations based on professional values can co-exist. It is likely that ethical questions will continue to be raised in connection with the practice of infant adoption in this country. Rising costs, increasing competition, and persistent socioeconomic inequities highlight the market dynamics that are likely to continue to raise questions about the nature of infant adoption as a service.

Part II

Market Forces: The Issues in International Adoption

Perspectives on international adoption, in relation to the role of market forces in shaping its nature and scope, generally fall into two categories. First is the view that international adoption provides children without families who are living in deplorable conditions in poor countries with loving families in more affluent countries [Berger 1995; Triseliotis 1993]; the opposing view is that international adoption creates an environment that fosters exploitation, the selling of children, and corruption [Hermann & Kasper 1992; Triseliotis 1993]. Both perspectives, as different as they may be in their overall assessment of international adoption, explicitly recognize market issues—specifically the differentials in power and resources that underlie intercountry adoption. The first perspective—which views international adoption in a highly positive way—frames its benefits in the successful placement of children in socially and economically disadvantaged environments with families who have superior financial and material advantages. The second perspective—which highlights the negative outcomes associated with international adoption—characterizes the intercountry placement of children in the darkest of market terms.

The tensions associated with market characterizations of international adoption relate, at least in part, to the range of circumstances that constitute international adoption practice. Hermann and Kasper [1992, pp. 47–48] note that for many children in developing countries, adoptions by families in more developed countries occur under clear circumstances evidencing children's legal availability for adoption, and represents for children "their only hope for a family or for surviving malnutrition or disease." They point to the worsening problem of poverty in India, for example, where family planning is not extensively used and large numbers of children are abandoned because their parents cannot afford to care for them. Such situations suggest that for the individual children involved, international adoption is a vital service while, at the same time, they raise issues regarding the economic and social inequities that underlie international adoption even in the most appropriate of circumstances.

In contrast to situations in which children do not have family who can raise them or opportunities for new families in their birth countries and who are placed with families in other countries through a regulated process, there are circumstances in which international adoption occurs in a highly questionable manner. Serious concerns have arisen about a range of international adoption practices, many of which came to light in the 1980s and some of which have continued to the present. Specifically, criticisms have focused on international adoption practices involving payments of sums to "adoption agents" in countries of origin to locate children for prospective adoptive parents [see Halbfinger 1999]; kidnaping of children for purposes of adoption [Cantwell 1983]; direct and meager payments to poor birth parents for their children [Cantwell 1983]; solicitation of women in public hospitals immediately after they give birth to convince them that adoption will give their children a better life [Cantwell 1983; Pastor 1989]; and bribes—in the form of money, trips abroad, or office equipment such as fax machines—to military officials and other authorities who then provide illegal papers for children who are made available for adoption [Children's Clarion 1987; Cummings 1998].

These blatant abuses—which, depending on the nature of the activity and the country, may or may not constitute illegal activity but which, nonetheless, raise troubling questions about international adoption—have led to criticisms of international adoption expressed in terms of that service as a "business." Does the very term "business" when applied to international adoption have negative implications? Or is the notion of international adoption as a "business" simply a reality that must be accepted? If there is a legitimate business component, are there nevertheless aspects of international adoption that reflect socially, legally, and/or ethically unacceptable practices?

The role of international adoption in benefiting individual children who do not have birth families or opportunities for family in their countries of origin is a critical factor that must be recognized in any analysis of international adoption. At the same time, there are justified concerns about some features of contemporary international adoption practice. As Tyree [1999, p. 1] notes:

> Few would argue that in most cases international adoption improves children's lives. It is also apparent, however, that international adoption has become big business in recent years, and in some countries, the system has become susceptible to corruption.

The following discussion focuses on the market forces associated with international adoption that have raised concerns—the growing demand for children from abroad; the role of money in international adoption; the extent to which abuses and exploitative activities occur in the international arena and how it shapes both the perception and reality of international adoption; differentials in power and resources between those who adopt and those who place their children and the power held by those who arrange international adoptions; and the role of oversight and regulation in current and future international adoption practice.

Demand and the Role of Money

The characterization of international adoption as a "business" is associated with worldwide perceptions of the growing demand in the United States and Europe for children to adopt, a demand that increasingly is bringing prospective adoptive parents to international adoption. Although adoption professionals note that there are far more children in orphanages and institutional settings around the world than there are families wishing to adopt them—Adamec [1999], for example, estimates some 250,000 children residing in Russian orphanages alone—international adoption often has not focused on these children. Instead, the perception and, to some degree, the reality is that prospective adopters from the United States and Europe see in international adoption the opportunity to readily "adopt the healthiest, brightest babies" in other countries—whether they are in orphanages or are available for adoption through other avenues [Cummings 1998].

The relative shortage of healthy newborns domestically and the lengthy wait for a baby of the prospective adopter's preferences in the U.S. and Europe have triggered a demand which, according to some, focuses on the "best" babies that other countries have to offer [Cummings 1998]. A U.S. humanitarian aid volunteer in Russia, for example, has observed, "We are taking out the kids that have the highest chance of surviving in their own culture, and we're leaving the ones that have the least chance" [Cummings 1998, p. 3]. He described Americans as "shopping for a child as if they were going into Wal-Mart looking for an item of clothing," with Russian children who have the "gold coin of beauty and silver coin of intelligence" promptly "snatched up" [Cummings 1998, p. 3]. Similarly, criticisms have been expressed of international adoption practice in Latin America where the more desirable children—in terms of age, health, and racial background—are made available to adopters from other countries and harder-to-place children remain in their countries of origin, often with few, if any, prospects for adoptive families [Kennard 1994; Pahz 1988]. Carro [1995, p. 136] notes that "adoptive parents are seen as wealthy window-shoppers, willing to spend any amount of money in order to buy a perfect baby."

It is important to note that as pervasive as this characterization may be in some circles, it does not apply to all individuals desiring to adopt children from other countries. Tyree [1999, p. 3], for example, quotes adoption professionals who describe some parents who adopt internationally as wanting to "do something to help" orphaned children living in socially or economically disadvantaged countries. Their desire to adopt may not be based on an urgent need for a baby but on altruistic motives, which may include a desire to rescue children from desperate conditions abroad. The nature of this altruism, however, may raise issues of its own, as reflected in the remarks of one adoptive parent of a child from Russia, who described Russian and Eastern European children as "born into societies that don't protect individuals, have no element of humanity in the responsibility of parents, and can't provide adequate schooling and health care" [cited in Tyree 1999, p. 5]. These parents may not be in the "mad scramble" for a baby as described by Gritter [1999, p. 11], but may find themselves in the midst of efforts to adopt that, as with those who seek the "perfect baby," come at increasingly higher costs.

The Cost of International Adoption

With the growing demand for children and the urgency that many prospective adopters feel to find healthy, attractive babies, increasing sums of money have become part of international adoption. Rios-Kohn [1998, p. 7] observes that "with so many families eager to adopt from other countries, adoptions have become a lucrative business." At one end of the spectrum are illegal activities, which involve the direct exchange of large sums of money for children. Some point to the "thriving black market" that has developed in some countries, in which significant sums of money exchange hands [Rios-Kohn 1998, p. 7]. In a 1995 report to the United Nations [Calcetas-Santos 1995], the special rapporteur noted the clandestine and illegal nature of some intercountry adoptions and the escalating profitability of these adoptions that has transformed them into a highly successful business ventures. "Dubious go-betweens in some poor countries take advantage of the rising demand for adopted children to relieve wealthy couples, tired of waiting for offspring of their own, of huge sums" [Jacot 1999, p. 2].

At the same time, larger sums of money have come to be associated with international adoption even when there are no apparent illegalities involving the direct exchange of money for children. One director of adoption services, noting the market forces shaping international adoption even when it is practiced at the most reputable level, has observed, "There are some real tensions now between the child focus and the consumer orientation, the human service model and the market forces. Some families start looking for the cheapest, the fastest, the 'we promise you a child that meets your quote-unquote specifications in so many months'" [cited in Mansnerus 1998, p. A17].

There is agreement within the international adoption community that the cost of international adoption has soared [Evans 1999; Bouwma 1999; Holtan 1999]. On average, the cost of adopting a child from another country ranges from $9,000 to $20,000 but depends on the country and the requirements related to travel or residence in the country of origin for completion of the adoption [Robinson 1996]. Although the adoption of a Russian child, for example, may well fall within this general range, the adoption of a child from Haiti may cost significantly less, averaging between $3,100 and $7,200 [Jacoby 1996]. On the other hand, there are instances of far higher fees for individual adoptions—ranging as high as $60,000 [Jacot 1996], a sum that raises the question whether at this level the threshold between legal and illegal activity has indeed been crossed.

The reasons advanced for the escalation in the cost of international adoption are varied. Some relate the increase in costs to greater professionalization of international adoption services in response to the demands of prospective adoptive parents [Evans 1999]. Evans [1999] points out that international adoption has become primarily a service for adoptive parents as the principal clients and that international adopters—with high levels of education and income and, often, political connections—have very high expectations related to the quality and responsiveness of international adoption services. At the same time, she notes that in addition to fees for professional services, there are increased costs associated with greater regulation by U.S. authorities, travel, translation, and other document-related services, and technological support [Evans 1999]. Requirements that prospective adoptive parents travel to children's home countries have become more commonplace, adding expense to the process. Holtan [1999] notes that some countries of origin have come to appreciate the financial benefits that flow to local economies as a result of these visits by adopting families.

Bouwma [1999] points out that the increasing cost of international adoption also is associated with the growing number of adoption agencies attempting to do business in other countries. Agencies have proliferated in Russia, Eastern Europe, and China, establishing programs in the absence of significant restrictions on the number of agencies that may qualify to make international adoption placements or requirements that they meet certain criteria—rigorous or otherwise—to do business in those countries [Bouwma 1999]. Others share Bouwma's concern that the number of U.S.-based international adoption agencies working in Eastern European and Asian countries has grown beyond a manageable level [Evans 1999; Tyree 1999]. Tyree [1999, pp. 1- 2] notes that international adoption has "created a multitude of jobs, especially in the United States, where hundreds of international adoption agencies have been launched," and that more than 80 agencies are active in Russia. More than 150 U.S. agencies currently have international adoption programs in China [Evans 1999]. The growing number of agency programs in these countries and others has led to increased competition and the need for each agency to position itself as able to provide the most desirable children in the most expeditious manner—for higher fees.

Finally, some commentators place at least some responsibility for increased costs on the conduct of prospective adoptive parents. Ortiz [1994, p. 39], in her analysis of market forces impacting Paraguayan adoptions, for example, has pointed to the willingness of adoptive parents to pay large sums of money and work with unscrupulous in-country facilitators who promise desirable results. She writes that prospective adoptive parents from other countries are willing to pay between $15,000 and $20,000 to adopt children from Paraguay and, in addition, are willing to place themselves in questionable situations in order to adopt. Upon arriving in Paraguay, adoptive parents must live four to five weeks with the child placed with them. Although these parents often reside in "the best hotels," she writes that they are "at their lawyer's mercy" in a country in which they are unfamiliar with the environment, the law, or the language [Ortiz 1994, p. 39]. "The dependence grows daily and does not end until a few hours before embarking on the plane—a situation which is well taken advantage of by the lawyers who are making the business" [Ortiz 1994, p. 39].

Situations in this country indicate that some prospective adoptive parents are willing to pay large sums of money to adopt internationally, even when there are signs that an adoption is being handled in an illegal or improper manner. Such willingness to overlook obvious improprieties was evident in a recent case involving the arrest of two New York women and an Arizona attorney for smuggling Mexican babies into the U.S. for adoption and charging their adoptive parents $20,000 each. The journalist, raising questions about the circumstances surrounding the adoptive placements of these children, rhetorically asked:

> Why would adoptive parents accept a baby from the two women in the parking lot of the 7-Eleven on Long Island, or from Mr. Reyes at a gas station on the Arizona side of the border? Why would the adoptive parents believe a claim that Mexican law allowed a parent to pick up the baby first and take care of paperwork later? [Allen 1999, p. B5].

Money and International Adoption Practice: The "Black Market" and the "Gray Market"

Because of the range of circumstances involved in international adoption, the role that money plays in any given adoption varies greatly. Although it may be tempting to conceptualize the range of practice in stark terms—as either the outright illegal selling of children or clearly legal and ethical practices—international adoption practices fall across a spectrum of activities between these extremes to include so-called "gray" market activities.

It is not clear to what extent clearly illegal practices play a role in international adoption, although such activities frequently are highlighted in the literature and in analyses of market forces in international adoption. International organizations, which primarily focus on situations in which human rights have been violated or illegal activities have taken place, have tended to highlight the most egregious aspects of international adoption practice. UNICEF [UNICEF International Child Development Centre 1998], for example, has outlined as the principal abuses in international adoption:

- *Illegally obtaining children for adoption.* Abduction of children; inducing young, unmarried mothers to place their children for adoption; falsely informing mothers that their children have died or were stillborn; offering women financial incentives to conceive a child for an intercountry adoption; exchange of a child for financial or material rewards; and providing false information to prospective adoptive parents.

- *Illegally securing permission to adopt.* Falsifying or falsely obtaining birth certificates and corruption of local officials and judges to obtain favorable decisions.

- *Illegally avoiding the adoption process.* Making false birth or paternity declarations and taking a child through a third country.

The extent to which these abuses occur has not been well documented, in large part because of their surreptitious nature. Some believe, however, that the types of activities described by UNICEF represent isolated occurrences or simply reflect traditional practices that characterize the way "business" is done in a given country. Bartholet [1996], for example, disputes the extent and impact of any abuses, arguing that such situations occur infrequently and that international adoptions are being unfairly misrepresented as "trafficking" when they are conducted in an essentially legal manner. Bartholet [1996, p. 200] writes:

When one looks beneath the surface of most media and other stories of child trafficking, it becomes clear that the

term "trafficking" is used very loosely. The stories sometimes involve claims that what is characterized as a
'bribe' has been paid to an official, without disclosing the
fact that small payments are traditional in the conduct of
all official business in the country at issue. Often the
trafficking headlines involve stories that reveal no more
than that the adoptive parents paid a good deal of money
to agencies or other adoption intermediaries, without
indicating that anything beyond legitimate fees for services were involved. Rarely is there any evidence that
birth parents have been paid, or that children have been
taken from birth parents capable of and interested in
raising them.

Her contention that birth parents of children adopted internationally are simply incapable of or uninterested in raising
their own children will be discussed later in this volume. Her
assertions that the exchange of "a good deal of money" for a
child is the equivalent of a "legitimate fee" and that bribes are
simply traditional payments, presumably involving little more
than pocket change, suggest that there is little reason for
concern regarding such payments. Her assessment of these
issues is undermined, however, by continuing reports of international adoption activities that are likely to meet even the
strictest definition of "trafficking."

A series of troubling revelations recently surfaced regarding
international practice, which, though not representative of the
practice as a whole, nonetheless suggest a legitimate basis for
concern. Two exposés involved the international adoption of
Vietnamese children. In one situation, 14 Vietnamese individuals
were arrested in Hanoi for buying children from poor families,
paying up to $70 a child, and selling them to individuals in other
countries for $1,000 to $1,500 [Buffalo News 1999]. It was estimated that the group had made a profit of approximately $700,000
over a four-year period [Buffalo News 1999]. On the heels of this
exposé were revelations regarding criminal "gangs" operating
international adoption networks in Vietnam. Members of one

such gang were arrested for buying 200 children from poor families and selling them to foreigners at a high profit—a situation that led the French government to suspend French citizens' adoptions of Vietnamese children until a fail-safe vetting procedure could be developed [Henley 1999]. Similar revelations surfaced in India where infants—principally girls between one month and one year of age—were rescued after being held by baby brokers posing as social workers. These individuals had bought babies from poor families for between $47 and $70 and charged adoptive parents from other countries between $2,000 and $3,000 to adopt them [BBC News 1999]. Similarly, a few years ago, charges were brought against a ring of lawyers and baby nurseries in Honduras who were accused of kidnapping babies and removing them to "fattening centers," where they were released for adoption after gaining weight and better health [Carro 1995].

On a less organized level, other incidents have involved the arrest of individuals in certain Latin American countries who were engaged in baby trafficking. Such activities have been uncovered in Peru—where an American attorney was arrested for falsifying birth records, bribing judges, and paying poor mothers as little as $5 for children—and in Brazil—where attention focused on an incident in which a pregnant woman was allegedly kidnapped, and her labor induced and who then was set free, without her baby [Carro 1995]. In Guatemala, it was discovered that in several cases, babies had been placed for adoption by women who had been paid to misrepresent themselves as the children's birth mothers [Jacot 1996]. This discovery led to requirements by Canada and the U.S. that accredited doctors conduct DNA tests to ensure the biological relationship between the child and the "parent" surrendering the child for adoption [Jacot 1996]. Although not indicative of the general practice of international adoption, these serious aberrations are of sufficient magnitude to raise a host of concerns and promote suspicions about international adoption.

Suspicions and fears regarding intercountry adoption and the potential abuses associated with this practice have been expressed

in their most extreme form in "body parts" rumors that periodically surface in relation to the adoption of children by "foreign"
families. Carro [1995, p. 137] notes that the rumor that children
adopted by U.S. and European families were serving as "living
organ banks" began in 1987 and rapidly spread throughout the
world. Believed by some to be a deliberate disinformation cam-
paign by the Soviet Union against the United States [Carro 1995],
the "baby parts" rumor took on apparent credibility as it was
repeated by the media and political and religious authority figures
in Honduras, Switzerland, the Netherlands, Canada, and Italy
[Carro 1995]. The United States attempted to dispel the rumor, and
although U.S. authorities believed that the charges had been
wholly discredited [United States Information Agency 1994],
others assert that such efforts have not been successful and
continue to impact perceptions of international adoption [Carro
1995]. In a recent resurgence of the rumor, members of the Russian
Duma expressed concerns about the "baby business" associated
with the international adoption of Russian children and asserted
that children were being sold for their organs—despite the absence of any evidence that such abuses were occurring [Cummings
1998]. The "body parts" rumors have been buttressed in some
countries by charges that children were being adopted by families
for other heinous purposes—including sexual abuse, the subjec-
tion of children to Satanic rituals, and their use as drug couriers
[Children's Clarion 1987].

The notion of profit-making ventures for children's body
parts or other purposes designed to exploit vulnerable children
from economically depressed countries has had remarkable en-
durance. What supports these ongoing concerns? Is it the amount
of money that has come to typify international adoption—sums
that are so significant that it becomes easy to assume that there
must be an ulterior and unsavory purpose? Is there a perception
that "foreign" families could not possibly love these children as
their own—and therefore must be using them to improve the lot of
their biological children (through use of their adopted children's
organs) or to better their own economic situation (through organ
sales or drug-related activities)?

Aside from obvious illegalities in international adoption involving trafficking in children and the issues related to abuse and exploitation are "gray market" issues involving the exchange of large sums of money which, though not in direct violation of laws prohibiting the outright sale of children, raise troubling questions. One example is the tradition of bribing officials in other countries to complete adoptions [Evans 1999]. Bribery of Russian officials has become an issue on which attention has focused. Tyree [1999], for example, reports the experience of one adoptive parent in Russia who was advised to bring $1,000 to Moscow for "gifts." Oleck [1999, p. 1] describes her own experience adopting from Russia in which her adoption agency advised her to bring $11,000 in cash and told her expressly "not to ask [Russian officials] where the money was going." This practice raises important ethical issues. Is bribery appropriate in international adoption when it reflects the way "business" is done in a country? Is it acceptable because it is necessary to ensure the desired outcome? Should it matter that bribes are paid because a child ultimately benefits—that is, a case of the end justifying the means? On the other hand, does the payment of bribes have an impact that transcends the individual transaction, affecting more broadly the character of international adoption? Tyree [1999, p. 4] notes the ambivalence that permeates the endemic practice of bribery in Russia:

> While it may be in the best interest of a child to be placed internationally, having rich Westerners throwing millions of dollars around to bypass bureaucracy is a very corrupting influence in a society that is struggling with a fragile democratic and free-market system.

"Gray market" concerns extend beyond bribery of officials in unregulated environments. Even in countries that closely regulate international adoption practice, there may be issues related to the charging of fees that raise troublesome questions. In China, for example, a $3,000 "orphanage donation" is charged to each adoptive parent. If a fee is required, is it a "donation"? Do these "donations" actually benefit the orphanages where children live?

If not, what exactly is the purpose of this additional sum of money paid by adoptive parents? Does its purpose matter if these "donations" are simply viewed as part of the cost of an adoption?

The Impact of Money on the Pool of Prospective Adoptive Families

A final issue related to the role of money in international adoption is the extent to which increasing costs have constricted the pool of potential adoptive families for the majority of children in need of families abroad—children in orphanages and other institutional settings. Particularly for children who are older or who have special needs, there is growing concern that the escalating cost of international adoption is seriously limiting their opportunities to be adopted. Holtan [1999], for example, observes that the very families who traditionally have adopted and successfully raised children with physical, mental health, and developmental problems may now be effectively "priced out" of the international adoption process. She [1999] notes that since the late 1960s and 1970s, children with special needs in this country primarily have been adopted by families of moderate means whose expectations for the children they adopt are consistent with the children's physical challenges, emotional fragility, and developmental delays. These moderate income families, however, are highly unlikely to have the financial resources that international adoption currently requires. As a consequence, children's opportunities to be adopted by families with characteristics strongly associated with positive adoptive outcomes have become increasingly limited [Holtan 1999].

The expectations of prospective adoptive parents who pay $20,000 or $30,000 to adopt internationally may be that the child they adopt will be a "good" one—that is, a child who is physically, intellectually, and developmentally attractive [Holtan 1999]. These families may expect high academic achievement, professional careers, and social success—outcomes that may not be realistic for children whose early institutional experiences have compromised their longer term potential. Holtan [1999] expresses concern that if international adoption is limited to affluent families with such expectations, a serious and painful mismatch between families and children may occur, giving rise to less than successful adoptions.

As noted earlier, federal policy designed to subsidize international adoptions through tax credits does not benefit families of moderate means as much as more affluent families who are able to initially absorb the substantial up-front cost of international adoption. Evans [1999] argues that the strengths and weaknesses of the tax credit approach, as applied to international adoption, should be examined carefully. Is there a commitment to supporting international adoption by all families or by only well-to-do families whose incomes allow them to benefit from a tax credit? Does a tax credit actually mitigate the costs of adoption or does it—as has been suggested by some—simply raise costs based on an assessment of what the market will bear? If the costs of international adoption simply track the benefits offered by tax credits, will the cost continue to rise, thereby pricing out some of the very families who can best provide for children with special needs?

International Adoption and Differentials in Power and Resources

In connection with the increasing role of money in international adoption are questions related to power and resource allocation—as they relate to women in countries of children's origin and the children themselves. Is undue pressure being exerted to force women in developing countries to place their babies for adoption? Are women being induced to have babies specifically for the purpose of international adoption? Do facilitators and adoption professionals—who most directly benefit financially from international adoption—take advantage of the dire economic status of many women in developing countries?

It is not clear to what extent international adoption places pressures on poor women to place their children for adoption with families from abroad. Such risks may be greater in some countries than in others. The United Nations, for example, recently began an investigation into international adoption practice in Guatemala in response to a host of complaints regarding lawyers' activities in arranging independent adoptions. The charges under investigation include the use of force to convince women to place their children for adoption and deceptive activities to induce women to consent to adoption, accompanied by the payment of excessively high fees by adoptive parents [Associated Press 1999]. It is asserted that lawyers have charged fees ranging between $3,000 and $30,000, while providing birth mothers with only approximately $100 in assistance [Associated Press 1999].

There have been charges since the 1980s that poor women have been pressured to have babies in order to place them for adoption. Pastor [1989], for example, claimed that young women in Honduras were being paid to become pregnant, provided with healthy diets and prenatal care, and then expected to place their children for adoption. "Once a baby is born and if the baby is healthy, the mother is paid $50.00 for the product. This practice is not very different from what we call 'surrogate motherhood' in the U.S.; however, it is substantially cheaper" [Pastor 1989, p. 19]. The notion that mothers of children adopted internationally essentially function as surrogates has been used to underscore what many see as the ongoing exploitation of poor women as "breeders" for affluent families in Western countries. The author of *Babies for Sale* [Neubauer 1988], for example, argues that, compared to an average of $10,000 generally associated with a surrogate motherhood situation in the U.S., a birth mother in Latin America or Asia receives "a pittance," estimated to translate into as little as $55 in U.S. dollars.

Another facet of this issue is presented by recent media coverage of organized efforts to transport poor pregnant women from other countries to the United States so that they may deliver their babies in this country and place them for adoption. In one case, attorneys were charged with bringing pregnant Russian women to Louisiana to deliver their babies and then place them for adoption [Ruane & Shaver 1998]. It was alleged that the women returned home to Russia with between $7,000 and $8,000 for their children, and that the attorneys charged adoptive parents as much as $42,500 for their services in arranging these adoptions [Ruane & Shaver 1998]. In a second case, a California-based lawyer was arrested and charged with allegedly smuggling as many as 40 poor Hungarian women into the U.S. and assisting them in placing their children with adoptive families ["Lawyer accused" 1999]. In this case, it was alleged that when women were not able to obtain U.S. visas, they were brought first into Canada and then slipped across the border into the U.S. to deliver and place their babies for adoption ["Lawyer accused" 1999].

There appears to be a strong relationship between the limited social and economic power of women in developing countries and the practice of international adoption. It is clear that poverty and low social status typify the backgrounds of the women who place their children for adoption internationally. Pilotti's study [1993] of the demographic characteristics of Latin American birth mothers who consented to the international adoptions of their children, for example, found that economic and social disadvantage uniformly characterized their backgrounds. Birth mothers were found to be young—between the ages of 14 and 18; poor; unemployed or active in the informal sector as street vendors, beggars, or prostitutes; poorly educated; and from neglectful or abusive home environments. Although some characterize the women who place their children for adoption as simply lacking the capability to rear their children [see Bartholet 1996], such incapacity, in reality, appears to be more closely associated with economic and social distress than with parenting ability or interest. Defense of Children International, an organization that has studied intercountry adoption, for example, concluded that "the vast majority [of birth parents] do not part with their children for money, but out of despair or with the hope to ensure the child's welfare or survival" [Lücker-Babel 1990, p. 2]. Others point to the extreme economic distress of parents in developing countries that may make international adoption appear to be the only viable option. Jacot [1996, p. 4], for example, quotes a Peruvian adoption official:

> Many mothers come to us because they want to give up a
> child they can no longer afford to bring up. We do all we
> can to dissuade them and help them. But here, as else-
> where, the first thing to do is to stem the tide of poverty.

Perry [1998, p. 105] notes that these realities have led to a
"troubling dilemma in international adoption: in a sense, the
access of affluent white Western women to children of color for
adoption is often dependent upon the continued desperate circumstances of women in Third World nations."

The economic and social distress of parents in developing
countries raise questions related to the nature of the decision-
making process leading to international adoptive placements.
These issues particularly arise in relation to the benefits and risks
associated with direct arrangements between prospective adoptive parents and birth parents and with arrangements made through
government supervised processes. To what extent do international adoptions arranged directly with birth mothers and made
possible through voluntary relinquishment heighten the danger of
exploitation ? Given the greater safeguards when children reside
in orphanages and their adoptions are arranged through a supervised process [Bouwma 1999], what accounts for the continued
high level of interest in direct arrangements with birth parents?
Bouwma [1999] observes that there is a clear risk of exploitation
in facilitator-arranged voluntary relinquishments leading to international adoptions. Options, particularly the possibility of providing assistance to the mother so that she can raise her child, are
not likely to be explored, and instead, adoption is offered as the
only solution in situations typically involving economic desperation. Bouwma also notes, however, that in countries where such
independently arranged adoptions are allowed, direct arrangements with birth mothers provide a more rapid—and, therefore,
more desirable—route for prospective adoptive parents than does
working with an orphanage, which often involves greater bureau-
cracy. As a consequence, independently arranged voluntary relinquishments—with the benefits of speed and the availability of

very young children—have come to be the favored approach despite the risks to birth parents that may be involved.

The realities associated with the conditions in developing countries from which children come may extend beyond the impact on poor women. Hermann and Kasper [1992, p. 47] argue that because of long-standing imbalances of power in international adoption, those who are vulnerable—both women and children—are at considerable risk of exploitation. They [1992, p. 47] write:

> Children are commodities. Throughout history, they have been bought, sold, and traded at the whim of adults. Both women and children experience the oppression that result from their financial, emotional and physical dependence on others. For this reason, their experiences in the realm of international adoption are similar. International adoption operates within a male-dominated system that is based on the laws and expectations of men.

They [1992, p. 55] also contend that the women who adopt children are likewise affected by the inequities of international adoption practice:

> The questions related to the rights of the woman who adopts, the rights of the birth mother, and the rights of the adopted child must be framed within the national and global implications and realities of sexism and the oppression of children. The political imperative to take these factors into account is clear from ethical, professional, moral and legal standards of conduct [1992, p. 56].

The issues related to differentials in resources and power, like the issues associated with the role of money in international adoption, raise critical questions regarding the regulation of international adoption practice. What is the role of regulation in a global marketplace? To what extent can regulation address the most negative effects of the market forces characterizing international adoption?

Regulation of International Adoption

The issues that arise in relation to market forces are closely associated with the regulation—or lack of regulation—of inter-country adoption. As international adoption has become a more acceptable form of creating families and has become more lucrative for many adoption practitioners, new agencies "from charitable, church affiliated agencies to walkup offices run by people who make money change hands in Bulgaria" have proliferated [Mansnerus 1998, p. A17]. There is general—though not uniform—agreement that few controls or systems are in place to regulate many aspects of their practice. Cummings [1998, p. 5] quotes William Pierce, former president for the National Council for Adoption, as stating that, although adoption agencies are regulated by the states in which they operate, the process is "virtually meaningless" and the field of international adoption is "getting worse" in this regard. Others, however, disagree. Bartholet [1996, p. 199], for example, maintains that "current law makes it extremely risky for adoption intermediaries and would-be adopters to engage in baby buying or kidnapping" and thus contends that it is not a process about which regulatory concerns should dominate.

The actual extent to which international adoption is subject to regulation and control is likely to be situated somewhere between Pierce's and Bartholet's views. UNICEF [1998, p. 7] has observed that regulation of international adoption is highly variable, depending on the country of children's origin and the circumstances surrounding the process in a given place and at a given time:

> Abuses in intercountry adoption are, not surprisingly, more likely in countries where there are no effective legislation and administrative structures and/or no coherent and workable child and family welfare policy.

Abuses are especially prevalent in 'private' adoptions and during periods of armed conflict, natural disasters, socio-political upheaval and economic crisis.

A review of the literature suggests that five factors play a role in the level of regulation of international adoption: (1) the acceptance of "private adoption" arrangements in some countries; (2) the absence of regulatory controls in some countries of origin; (3) the absence of standards that govern U.S. agency practice in children's birth countries; (4) limited regulation of international adoption practice in the U.S. at the state level; and (5) the absence of international consensus on standards of practice.

"Private" adoptions. "Private" international adoptions are often associated with abuse because such adoptions tend to take place outside of any existing regulatory systems [UNICEF 1998]. In a number of Latin American countries, independent facilitators readily act as adoption intermediaries and expedite international adoptions in ways that have raised concerns about the potential for exploitation. In Guatemala, as one example, attorneys work independently of the state system, despite the fact that the law requires international adoption agencies to work with attorneys in finalizing adoptions [Evans 1999]. An extremely simple process exists for the taking of voluntary relinquishments: a notary obtains the consent of one or both of the child's birth parents; the lawyer for the adoptive parents presents the completed document and a social worker's report to a judge; and the judge approves the adoption [Jacot 1996]. This process has been criticized as making it far too easy to pressure or blackmail a birth mother into placing her child for adoption because birth parents are usually poor and illiterate, and lawyers, notaries, and social workers involved in the process often work in collusion [Associated Press 1999; Jacot 1996].

There appears to be agreement that abuses in international adoption are more likely when adoptive parents work with independent adoption agents—often unlicensed brokers who facilitate the adoption process within the child's country—to avoid what they perceive as bureaucratic complications [Bouwma 1999; Carstens & Julia 1995; Evans 1999]. The opportunity for financial

gain on the part of these intermediaries may be ripe at each stage of
the adoption process because of the direct dependence of prospective
adoptive parents on these individuals [Carstens & Julia 1995; Ortiz
1994]. Intermediaries predisposed to maximizing the financial return on international adoptions, however, are not confined to developing countries. The recent case involving two suburban housewives
in New York and their lawyer-colleague in Arizona who smuggled
Mexican babies into the U.S. to place them with adoptive families for
high fees reflects the relative ease with which independent brokers
may operate in this country [see Allen 1999].

   ***Legislation, administrative structures, and policy in
children's countries of origin.*** Experts appear to be in accord
that it is in children's countries of origin that the development of
legislative, administrative and regulatory controls is critical
[Bouwma 1999; Evans 1999; Holtan 1999]. Models for such practice are found in South Korea and China whose highly regulated
systems have well-established guidelines regarding the amount of
money to be charged, the time frame for adoption, and the format
for completing an adoption—systems, which Evans [1999] notes,
are commendable for "the relative transparency of the process."
By contrast, some countries in Latin America and Eastern and
Central Europe have few regulatory controls in place or poorly
enforce existing regulations or official policy—features that support a "survival of the fittest" environment benefitting those most
skilled at maximizing financial opportunities [Bouwma 1999]. In
many countries, the development and enforcement of regulatory
controls have not been a priority [Bouwma 1999]. In other countries, the existence of any regulatory process is periodically
undermined by complete changes in government [Cox 1999]. As
a consequence of the relative dearth of governmental oversight in
certain countries—in the form of either legislative or administrative controls—exploitative practices have been able to thrive
[Bouwma 1999; Evans 1999].

   U.S. agency practice in children's countries of origin.
Adequate regulation of international adoption is an issue, even
given the greater protections against abuse and exploitation asso-

ciated with adoption agencies. In this connection, agency practice has been subject to particular criticism with regard to their relationships with facilitating agents in children's countries of origin [Evans 1999]. The agency-facilitator relationship traditionally has been based on "good faith," but Evans [1999] notes that agencies may now be operating on "blind faith" in an environment in which international adoption has grown rapidly and the financial return has escalated. As agencies open new programs in other countries, they may enter into relationships with independent facilitators whose backgrounds they do not thoroughly investigate [Evans 1999].

Because the quality and integrity of facilitators in children's countries of origin vary significantly [Bouwma 1999; Evans 1999], agencies may face ethical dilemmas in their work with these individuals. Facilitators, for example, initially may engage in highly reputable practice, but alter their methods and increase the charges for their services in response to perceived market opportunities. Experts report experiences in which facilitators significantly inflate the charges for their services in response to perceptions of what the market will bear or engage in what is described as "shopping around," that is, offering a healthy baby to the highest agency bidder [Bouwma 1999; Evans 1999]. Because prospective adoptive parents are increasingly willing to pay higher fees to secure a young healthy child within a short period of time, facilitators in children's countries of origin have come to recognize the added value of their services and charge accordingly [Bouwma 1999]. Having invested time and money in developing relationships with in-country facilitators, agencies may be reluctant to call facilitators to task when they engage in these and other troubling behaviors or to take steps to terminate those relationships [Hester 2000]. Many adoption professionals believe that quality international adoption practice is more likely to be achieved when agencies implement their own programs in children's countries of origin and hire their own staff. They also agree, however, that many agencies cannot afford to develop in-country programs and that it is likely that most agencies will continue to rely on independent facilitators in children's countries of origin [Evans 1999; Bouwma 1999].

Regulation of international adoption practice at the state level. The need for greater regulation of international adoption by state adoption regulators in the U.S. is an additional factor bearing on the quality of international adoption practice. In an analysis of issues related to the regulation of international adoption, Livingston identified the lack of uniformity in state adoption law "as one of the areas of greatest frustration for both state and federal officials involved in international adoption" [n.d., p. 41]. She found that most state laws had no legal definition of the "placement of a child for adoption;" failed to differentiate who may legally place children for adoption domestically and internationally; and gave broad latitude to a range of individuals who legally were allowed to "arrange" for adoptions [n.d., pp. 41-42]. She noted that these aspects of state adoption law allowed "unprincipled or inexperienced adoption arrangers [to] skirt the law by claiming that they are not 'placing' children [but] only 'arranging for adoption' or 'counseling' about adoption" [n.d., p. 42]. She [n.d., p. 42] described the troubling outcomes associated with ambiguities in state law:

> States which do not define "placement" generally find it difficult to regulate or penalize incompetent or unethical adoption arrangers or counselors since what they are doing is not regulated or defined by state law or regulations. Unregulated foreign adoption arrangers and counselors have been a significant factor in failed adoptions and financial exploitation of prospective adopters.

She [n.d., p. 43] also found that most state laws had no effective enforcement response even when it was clear that existing child placement and adoption agency regulations had been violated. In the majority of states, violation of child placing laws was a misdemeanor, and in several states, there was no penalty whatsoever [Livingston n.d.]. In the 11 states which made violations of child placement and adoption regulation a felony, she found that prosecution was rare [Livingston n.d.]. She [n.d., p. 45] concluded:

Obviously, systems with penalties that are not enforced do not significantly deter adoption-related fraud and incompetence. Systems without penalties do not deter at all . . . I find this . . . . ironic when compared with state laws pertaining to other state felony punishments . . . It is a sad commentary on our society that it is a more heinous crime in North Carolina to throw a piece of trash on a highway (punishable by a $1,000 fine) than to place a child illegally or in an unsuitable home in 41 states.

International consensus on standards of international adoption practice. At this point, consensus on international adoption practice has not been achieved, but greater regulation may be made possible through the Hague Convention on Inter-country Adoption. Signed by 50 countries, including the United States, and ratified by 38 countries (the United States not yet among them at the time of this writing), the Hague Convention is designed to serve as a protection for children, their birth parents, and adoptive parents. Among the provisions of the Hague Convention are mandates that each member country establish a "central authority" to oversee the accreditation of the providers of international adoption services, maintain oversight of the process, and account for the children entering its borders through international adoption. The Hague Convention also imposes controls in an attempt to curb excesses in the amount of money changing hands in international adoptions and to end the bribery and other exploitative activities which Oleck [1999] describes as "endemic" in the process, particularly in certain Latin American and Eastern European countries.

As of early 2000, the United States had not ratified the Hague Convention through federal implementing legislation. Although the U.S. signed the Convention in 1994—indicating its intent to ratify the treaty—a range of political considerations delayed both the introduction of federal implementing legislation and, even after bills were introduced in Congress in 1999, the enactment of a law that would bring the U.S. into compliance with the Convention's requirements. Issues related to power and accountability have played out in the form of contentious battles regarding the federal agency that would serve as the "central authority" for international adoptions (the Department of State versus the Department of Health and Human Services); disputes regarding which of several entities would be designated as an "accreditation body" with the power to determine which agencies could provide international adoption services; and arguments as to the respective positions of adoption lawyers and adoption agencies in the transaction of international adoptions.

It remains to be seen whether countries that ratify the Hague Convention will be able, through implementing treaty provisions, to bring an end to the most compelling concerns regarding international adoption: baby trafficking, the exploitation of impoverished women, and other unsettling aspects of international adoption which, as Oleck [1999, p. 2] notes, give children's birth countries "the jitters" and put all aspects of international adoption into question. The course of Hague Convention ratification in the U.S. suggests that the focus may be on issues bearing more on the consolidation of power and market position and less on accountability, particularly to children, birth families, and birth countries.

Intercountry Adoption and the Development of In-Country Child and Family Services

A final issue related to market forces in international adoption is the relationship between the resources that support international adoption and the resources that support the development of child and family services in children's countries of origin. Some maintain that Western countries—where most adoptive families reside—should assist developing countries to create and implement in-country child and family services rather than contributing to their economies through the international adoption of children. Serrill [1991, p. 86], for example, queries, "Why should millions of dollars be spent each year in the search for adoptive children . . . when the same money could be dispensed as foreign aid to help Third World children at home?" These arguments take note of the substantial economic boost that international adoption gives to children's countries of origins. Some experts have cited annual income streams from international adoptions at levels of $15-20 million in South Korea, $5 million in Guatemala, and $2 million in Honduras [Rothschild 1988; Kennard 1994]. Some assert that the provision of significant and much-needed financial resources to poorer nations through international adoption, although ostensibly supporting those countries' economies, has in reality promoted corruption and fraudulent practices [Kennard 1994].

A number of international adoption agencies based in the U.S. provide financial and technical assistance to children's countries of origin to assist them in building an infrastructure of services for children and families. Bouwma [1999] takes the position that support of in-country services is ethically required of agencies to strengthen families' abilities to raise their children and diminish the need to rely on international adoption. An example of such a program is the single parents program operated by Holt International Children's Services in Vietnam, which provides single mothers with financial support, vocational training, and job placement services [Dahl 1999]. In line with this type of programmatic effort, Serrill [1991, p. 8] quotes Cheri Register, an adoptive mother of two children from Korea, as observing:

> Wealth does not entitle us to the children of the poor. International adoption is an undeserved benefit that has fallen to North Americans, West Europeans and Australians, largely because of the inequitable socioeconomic circumstances in which we live. In the long run, we ought to be changing those circumstances.

Agencies, however, differ significantly in their commitment to in-country resource development. Because some agencies focus on maximizing the number of children they are able to place through adoption, they do not commit resources to the development of social services for birth families that could potentially reduce the pool of available∇and particularly desirable—children. The lack of provision of social service assistance to children's birth countries, however, may not impact the fees that agencies

charge. Ironically, many agencies that do not provide in-country social services charge adoptive parents higher fees than
agencies that provide such services [Bouwma 1999]. Bouwma
[1999] points out that the lack of agency willingness to provide
in-country support is not the only reason that such services may
be unavailable or extremely limited. China, for example, has
not accepted offers of assistance in developing social services,
suggesting cultural barriers to external support [Bouwma 1999].
Russia and Romania, by contrast, are characterized by environments in which the need for social services is "endless," as is
the cost of providing such services [Bouwma 1999], suggesting
that the need for in-country service development may be so
great that the efforts of individual agencies may seem too
minimal to be of relevance.

Another perspective on the relationship between intercountry adoption and support of in-country services is that the two
service areas are distinct and have no bearing on one another.
From this perspective, international adoption is not designed to be
a broad solution to the overall conditions affecting children in
developing countries and serves, at best, a small number of
children who would otherwise languish in institutional settings
[Serrill 1991]. In this view, international adoption "create[s] a
small safety valve in countries that have more people than they
can feed and house" [Serrill 1991, p. 86], and because of its limited
role, has little effect on whether child and family support programs are developed in countries in which children live. The
question of the role of international adoption in relation to support
of in-country child and family services remains open. It may be
that international adoption has not precluded the development of
in-country support services, but, at least according to some, it may
not have significantly supported the development of such programs either [Carstens & Julia 1995].

Summary

The market forces of international adoption raise a number of
questions with ethical implications. The field is confronted with

a host of difficult issues involving the growing demand for young children to adopt, the increased role of money in international adoption, and the marked differences in power and resources between those who adopt and those who place their children for adoption. The conflicting views of international adoption arise, in large part, from differing assessments of the extent to which these dynamics work in favor of or against the best interests of children. The negative perceptions of international adoption rest on concerns that children have become commodified, their birth parents have been exploited, and third parties have financially benefitted at the expense of children and families in developing countries. There are, however, more positive views of international adoption from a market perspective. Cox [1999] points out that the greater demand for and, consequently, heightened visibility of international adoption have led to a better understanding of international adoption as an opportunity for children and parents. The shrinking of the global community has made adoption across national boundaries more acceptable as a way of meeting the needs of children without families. At the same time, she notes that international adoption has led to greater cultural acceptance of adoption in children's birth countries and has promoted higher levels of in-country adoption. In the words of Mercedes Rosario de Martinez, founder of Colombia's Foundation for the Adoption of Abandoned Children, "this is not a business; it's devotion to the children. Because of that, the world is a better place" [cited in Serrill 1991, p. 86].

The disputes regarding international adoption are likely to continue. There will be those who continue to believe that "international adoption is often not the best alternative, and children are merely products of an elaborate system that sells them from the Third World to adults in developed nations" [Hermann and Kasper 1992, p. 49]. As expressed by Hermann and Kasper [1992, p. 50], there may be the sense that "although adoption may contribute to the well-being of tens of thousands of children, it may contribute to the continued oppression of tens of millions." On the other hand, there are those who are likely to agree with the observations of Carro [1995, p. 148]:

Legitimate intercountry adoption, based on the best interests of the child, should be recognized as beneficial for the adoptable children of sending countries as well as for the adopting parents of the receiving ones. If all of these local, regional and international efforts do succeed in eliminating the abuses, fear and mistrust that surround international adoption, then this practice will be perceived not as an abominable traffic human flesh but instead as what it should be—an act of love.

Part III

Market Forces in Foster Care and Adoption in the United States

Although not always recognized as having a "market forces" component, the adoption of children in foster care nonetheless presents issues related to the role of money, power, and accountability. In the paradigm of supply and demand, children in foster care waiting for adoptive families present the growing "demand" for which, historically, there has been an inadequate supply of adoptive families. As opposed to the high demand among adults for the relatively limited supply of infants, there is a relatively low level of interest among prospective adopters for the types of children typically in foster care: older children; children with special health, mental health, or developmental needs; sibling groups; and children of color who are of older age. The unmet needs of waiting children in foster care for adoptive families contrast sharply with the unmet needs of adults waiting for healthy children to adopt. The financial issues impacting this form of adoption also contrast starkly with infant and international adoption. The cost of adoption is generally quite limited, so that unlike adoptive parents who seek to adopt very young children, those who adopt children in foster care tend to be of moderate means and face few fiscal barriers to adopting initially. They, however, adopt children whose needs may require considerable financial resources into the future∇and the issue becomes the extent to which financial support is made available to these families as they parent children with special needs.

The following discussion explores the growing demand for adoption planning and services for children in foster care, particularly in relation to changes in federal welfare and child welfare policy and considers important supply-side considerations: the relationship between child demographics and adoptive family supply; the demographics of families who historically adopted and currently adopt children in foster care; and issues related to an effective expansion of the pool of adoptive families for this group of children. What role does money play in the adoption of children with special needs? To what extent are adoption subsidy benefits and postadoption services recognized as viable components of special needs adoption? What ethical considerations are raised by the dynamics of demand and supply in special needs adoption and the fiscal considerations that may drive policy and practice?

The Demand for Adoption Planning and Services

Historically, only about 15% of the 130,000 to 150,000 adoptive families formed each year are comprised of children formerly in foster care who are adopted by unrelated adults [Hollinger 1996; Flango & Flango 1995]. Until recently, the number of children adopted from foster care remained at a relatively constant level and represented an increasingly smaller proportion of children in foster care each year. Since the mid-1980s, the number of children in foster care has grown each year∇a trend that has continued to the present∇while the actual number of finalized adoptions, until the mid-1990s, remained in the range of 17,000 to 21,000 a year [Tatara 1993]. The U.S. Department of Health and Human Services (HHS) [2000] estimated in March 1999 that there were 547,000 children in care, an increase of approximately 80% in the number of children who were in care in FY 1987 [see Tatara 1993]. Until recently, the number of children in foster care who needed adoptive families was subject to only broad estimates, with states historically reporting that between 15% and 20% of the children in care needed families through adoption [McKenzie 1993]. The United States Department of Health and Human Services [2000] more specifically estimated in March 1999 that 117,000 of the children in foster care as of that date needed or would need adoptive families.

Poverty and the Growth in Foster Care and the Demand for Adoption Planning and Services

As is the case with many children adopted internationally, a large percentage of children in foster care∇and children who are wait-ing for adoptive families∇are from birth families who are poor [HHS 1996]. Research has consistently demonstrated that poverty is a critical factor in children's entry into foster care [Lindsey 1994]. Although abuse and neglect that pose an imminent risk of harm to a child are the legal and social work bases for the removal of children from their parents' custody [Myers 1992], some studies have found that unstable sources of parental income rather than the severity of child abuse account for many of the decisions to place children in foster care [Lindsey 1994; Pelton & Milner 1994]. Approximately one-half of all children in care come from families eligible for welfare benefits [U.S. House of Representatives 1996], and the majority of children who enter foster care do so because of poverty-related neglect or parental capacity associated with sub-stance abuse or mental illness [Courtney 1999]. The impact of poverty on foster care entry is heightened by its relationship with single parenting and ethnicity [Baugher & Lamison-White 1995], factors also associated with higher levels of foster care placements [U.S. House of Representatives 1996].

Recent policy developments suggest that poverty may be-come an even more compelling factor associated with children's entry into foster care and their subsequent need for adoption services. With the implementation of The Personal Responsibility and Work Opportunity Reconciliation Act of 1996 (P.L. 104-93) (popularly known as "welfare reform"), concerns have risen that poverty will precipitate an even greater increase in the number of child abuse and neglect referrals and, consequently, more chil-dren entering foster care; longer stays for children once they enter the child welfare system; and increases in the number of children freed for adoption. These concerns relate to a number of provi-sions in the law that are likely to have a substantial effect on children and families served through the child welfare system [HHS 1996]:

- The elimination of any individual entitlement to welfare assistance under Temporary Assistance to Needy Families (TANF), the program that replaced the Aid to Families with Dependent Children (AFDC) program;

- A five-year lifetime limit on cash assistance to needy families, although states may opt for a shorter time limit and may exempt up to one-fifth of their caseloads from the designated time limit;

- A requirement that states move families receiving assistance into work, with mandated work participation rates of 50% for single-parent families by 2002 and 90% for two-parent families by 1999;

- A life-time prohibition against the receipt of cash assistance or Food Stamp benefits by any individual convicted of a drug-related felony;

∞ The narrowing of the definition of childhood disability for purposes of children's eligibility for the Supplemental Security Income (SSI) program, a change anticipated to reduce the number of low-income children eligible for SSI by 315,000 by 2002 [Super et al. 1996]; and

- Significant reductions in the Food Stamp program, estimated to reduce the number of participants in the program by 20% [Super et al. 1996].

Data from states which made significant changes in their welfare programs prior to the enactment and implementation of federal "welfare reform" legislation suggest that reductions in welfare benefits to poor families result in increases in child protective services referrals. In Los Angeles County, for example, the number of child abuse and neglect referrals increased 12% when there was a 2.7% reduction in family welfare benefits, and referrals increased by 20% the following year when welfare benefits were again reduced by 5.8% [Children's Defense Fund 1997]. A recent analysis of the impact of federal welfare reform legislation indicated a substantial negative impact on family functioning, though no direct impact as of late 1998 on child protective services referrals [Children's Defense Fund & National Coalition for the Homeless 1998]. The analysis, nonetheless, suggested reason for concern regarding child and family well-being as a result of findings that only a fraction of the new jobs held by welfare recipients paid above-poverty wages; many families had lost income or had not found steady jobs despite the pressure to do so; and extreme poverty had grown more common for children, particularly children in working families and in female-headed households [Children's Defense Fund & National Coalition for the Homeless 1998].

Although the impact of welfare reform is yet to be fully realized [Child Protection Reports 1999], it is anticipated that poor families will be negatively affected by reductions in support as a result of time limits on cash assistance, non-compliance with work requirements, loss of eligibility for benefits because of drug-related offenses, and decisions by states to reduce or eliminate welfare benefits for economic or political reasons [Courtney 1999]. Given the existing linkage between poverty and foster care entry [Jones & McCurdy 1992; Pelton & Milner 1994], there may be a greater risk that children will enter care because of neglect-based factors. Parental inability to find work or effectively make use of education and training—which may trigger loss of welfare benefits—may well lead to child protective services intervention [Courtney 1999]. Similarly, the expansion of work requirements without provisions that ensure child care for program participants [Super et al. 1996] may pose for many poor families the dilemma of either complying with work requirements and leaving their children unsupervised, or foregoing work participation and losing financial assistance [Courtney 1999]. In New York City, for example, the City Administration recently proposed that homeless families in the city's shelter system who failed to work or meet other shelter or work requirements under TANF be subjected to the "loss of their children" through foster care placement [Bernstein 1999, p. B5].

As the effects of welfare reform-related stresses on families become more apparent, the extent to which deepening poverty will affect the length of children's stays in foster care also will become more evident [see Harper & Vandivere 1999]. It is important to note that analyses of the length of time children spend in foster care suggest that, even when AFDC supports were in place, children were remaining in care for extended periods of time [Goerge et al. 1994]. In its analysis of five states that together represent almost half of the population of children in foster care in the United States, Goerge and colleagues [1994] found that the median duration of first foster care stays for children ranged from a low of 8.7 months in Texas to a high of just under 3 years in Illinois. Federal data indicates that of March 31, 1998, almost one-fifth of the 520,000 children in foster care∇some 93,600 children∇ had been in care five or more years [U.S. Department of Health & Human Services 1999].

Should poverty cause even more children to enter foster care and remain in care longer, there likely will be difficulties reuniting children with their families. If families have lost financial support under TANF—which may be permanent in those cases in which time limits for benefits have been exhausted or in situations in which either parent has been convicted of a drug-related felony—families may lack the financial resources to establish and sustain a stable and safe home. Other families may face difficulties in regaining custody of their children if they have lost or experienced significant reductions in their Food Stamps benefits. For yet other families, their children may have lost SSI benefits, and as a result, no longer have access to medical and developmental services that their families, on their own, will not be able to provide.

Because of these potential consequences of welfare reform, the current challenges related to reunification of children with parents may be further exacerbated. It is unlikely that child welfare systems will be able to provide families with stable sources of income so that they may regain custody of their children. Nor can the system be reasonably expected to create access to health care and developmental services for uninsured children so that their families can resume responsibility for them. As a consequence, it can be anticipated that more children will have adoption as their permanency plan for poverty-based reasons, particularly given the time frames established by the Adoption and Safe Families Act (ASFA), P.L. 105-89, for termination of parental rights. This shift in service planning and delivery is likely to have a significant impact on child welfare agencies' resources. The budgetary implications of extended service delivery through adoption planning, adoption subsidies and postadoption servicesⱽwhich may be significant—are discussed later in this book.

Adoption Demand and the Adoption and Safe Families Act

Prior to the enactment and implementation of the Adoption and Safe Families Act in 1997, the number of children in foster care whose adoptions were finalized in any given year, as noted earlier, had remained quite stable despite the growth in the number of children in care. In FY 1982, between 22,000 and 24,000 adoptions of children in foster care were finalized [Tatara 1993], but for more than a decade thereafter, the number of adoptions finalized each year ranged between only 17,000 and 21,000 [Tatara 1993] . A shift became evident in FY 1997 when 31,000 adoptions of children in foster care were finalized [HHS 1999] and in FY 1998 when 36,000 adoptions were finalized [HHS 2000]. The upward trend may continue [Kroll 1999a]. These increases are associated with the recent policy emphasis on adoption for children in foster care, as perhaps most clearly articulated by the Adoption and Safe Families Act.

Enacted in 1997, the Adoption and Safe Families Act (ASFA) incorporated a number of new federal mandates, including requirements for more extensive use of termination of parental rights in the context of permanency planning for children in foster care. ASFA made two significant changes in federal law in this area in an effort to promote adoption as a permanent plan for children. First, ASFA set out certain circumstances under which "reasonable efforts" to reunify children in care with their birth families are not required and which, as a result, can set the stage for more quickly moving forward with termination of parental rights [42 USC §671 (a)(15)(D)]. These circumstances, which must be found by a court of competent jurisdiction, include:

1. The parent has subjected the child to "aggravated circumstances"—as defined by state law but which may include abandonment, torture, chronic abuse, and sexual abuse.

2. The parent has committed certain criminal acts: the murder or voluntary manslaughter of another child of the parent; attempt, conspiracy, solicitation or aiding and abetting in the murder or voluntary manslaughter of another child of the parent; or a felony assault that results in serious bodily injury to the child or another child of the parent.

3. The parent's rights to a sibling have been terminated involuntarily.

When a court of competent jurisdiction finds any of these circumstances, the child welfare agency must file a petition to terminate parental rights [42 USC §675(e)(4)(E)], although certain exceptions, discussed below, apply. Likewise, when a court of competent jurisdiction determines an infant to be abandoned, the agency must immediately file a petition for termination of parental rights [42 U.S.C. §675(e)(4)(E)]. Second, the law mandates the filing of a petition for termination of parental rights based on certain time considerations. Specifically, a petition must be filed when a child has been in foster care for 15 of the most recent 22 months [42 USC §675(e)(4)(E)]. In light of data that demonstrate the relatively long average stays of children in foster care [Goerge et al. 1994], it can be anticipated that this provision linking time in care with termination of parental rights will serve as the basis for a substantial proportion of the petitions to terminate parental rights.

The provisions to expedite termination of parental rights on the basis of time in care, parental commission of designated criminal acts, abandonment, and other bases related to child safety, however, are not absolute. ASFA [42 USC § 675(e)(4)(E)] provides three exceptions to the mandate that a petition to terminate parental rights be filed:

1. The state may opt not to file for termination of parental rights when the child is being cared for by a relative;

2. The state agency need not pursue termination of parental rights if it documents in the case plan a "compelling reason" that filing a termination of parental rights petition would not be in a child's best interests; and

3. In those cases in which "reasonable efforts" to reunify are required, the state agency is not required to file a termination of parental rights petition if it has not provided to the family the services necessary for the safe return of the child to them.

Despite these exceptions, it is anticipated that a growing number of children will be freed for adoption as larger numbers of petitions to terminate parental rights are filed and some portion of these petitions are granted [HHS 1999]. Federal data projections suggest that the population of children needing adoptive families has already expanded significantly because of ASFA requirements. The U.S. Department of Health and Human Services [2000] has estimated that one-fifth of the children in foster care in March 1999 had a permanency goal of adoption and of these children, 117,000 children were "waiting" to be adopted—a substantial increase in the 1993 estimate that 86,000 children in foster care were in need of adoptive families [McKenzie 1993].

Placements of children with adoptive families and finalizations of adoptions, however, will be dependent on factors other than ASFA mandates related to termination of parental rights. A key issue will be whether an adequate supply of adoptive families for these children can be recruited, prepared, and supported in the adoptions of these children—an issue highlighted by reported data that as of March 1999, 18,636 of the current population of waiting children (approximately 16%) were in preadoptive homes [HHS 2000]. The increases in the number of finalized adoptions in FY 1997 and 1998 may suggest that successful efforts at adoptive family recruitment and placements of children with adoptive families are under way. It may be more likely, however, that the FY 1997 and FY 1998 adoptions involved children already placed with adoptive families and for whom procedural, rather than placement, barriers had caused delays in adoption finalization. If the early increases in adoption rates are attributable principally to clearing procedural hurdles to adoption, significant challenges may remain with regard to adoptive family recruitment and preparation for the substantial number of waiting children.

The Supply: Adoptive Families for Children in Foster Care

Given the growing demand for adoption as a result of increasing numbers of children in foster care in need of adoption planning and services, the recruitment, preparation, and support of prospective adoptive families for children in foster care are likely to be critical issues for this population of children. From a market perspective, it has become clear that the supply of adoptive families for children in foster care awaiting adoption is not adequate. Who are the waiting children? What are the characteristics of families who historically have adopted children in foster care? To what extent can recruitment of a broad range of prospective adoptive families succeed in meeting the increased need?

Supply in Relation to the Nature of the Demand

An analysis of the supply of adoptive families for children in foster care necessarily involves an assessment of the extent to which there is a demographic "match" between children needing adoptive families and the characteristics of children generally sought by prospective adoptive parents. Three key factors that enter into this analysis are the age, race, and health status of the child.

Demographic data regarding children in foster care who are waiting for adoptive families indicate that these children tend to be older. As of March 31, 1999, very few waiting children were infants or toddlersⱯthe children most often sought by prospective adoptive parents [Mansnerus 1998]. Only 2% of the children awaiting adoptive families were less than one year old, and larger percentages were children between the ages of 1 and 5 years (35%), 6 and 10 years (37%), 11 and 15 years (23%), and 16 and 18 years (3%) [HHS 2000]. This age-related dynamic has an important impact on the adoption opportunities for waiting children as historically, it has been younger children in foster care who have been placed with adoptive families. In FY 1998, for example, almost half (48%) of all finalized adoptions were of children between birth and five years of age, with declining proportions of all finalized adoptions of children between the ages of 6 and 10 (37%), between 11 and 15 (14%), and between 16 and 18 (2%) [HHS 2000]. Predictably, very young children tend to have much shorter waits for adoptive families, and older children, conversely, are more likely to wait a prolonged period of time to be placed with adoptive families, if at all [Barth 1997].

The race of waiting children is a second demographic variable bearing on supply. The population of children in foster care and especially those waiting for adoptive families are disproportionately African American. Research indicates that African American children are proportionately far more likely to enter foster care than are Caucasian children. In 1990, the probability that an African American child would enter foster careⱯwhen compared to a Caucasian childⱯranged from 3 times greater in Texas to 10 times greater in New York than the probability that a Caucasian child would enter care [Goerge et al. 1994]. In that same year, more than 5% of the African American infants in Texas and New York lived in foster care at some point in time [Goerge et al. 1994]. As of March 1998, African American children—who comprise only 15% of the child population in the U.S. [U.S. Bureau of the Census

1998]—comprised 45% of the children in foster care [U.S. Department of Health and Human Services 1999].

Once in foster care, African American children, as well as other children of color, remain in care for longer periods of time than do Caucasian children [Goerge et al. 1995]. A recent study of children placed in foster care in New York City for the first time in 1992, for example, found that one-quarter of African American children were still in care as of January 1998 as compared to one-fifth of the Latino children and one-tenth of Caucasian children [Child Welfare Watch 1998]. Similarly, a study of length of stay for children of color in Washington State found that 20% of African American children and 22% of American Indian children remained in foster care for more than four years compared to 12% of Caucasian children [English & Clark 1996]. Given these statistical patterns, it is not surprising to find that data on the ethnic backgrounds of children waiting to be adopted reflects even greater disproportionality for African American children. As of March 1999, 51% of the waiting children were African American, compared to 32% who were Caucasian, and 11% who were Latino [HHS 2000].

The ethnicity of waiting children in foster care is a demographic factor with significant supply-side implications. Research demonstrates that women who seek to adopt are predominantly Caucasian women who pursue adoption because of infertility [Bachrach et al. 1991], and that, with the exception of a very small percentage of these women, they seek to adopt healthy white infants or toddlers [see Bachrach et al. 1991; Courtney 1997]. As the supply of Caucasian infants has decreased, there has been a greater willingness on the part of Caucasian adults to consider the adoption of African American infants [see Chandra et al. 1999]. In relation to adult demand for adoption, however, the research and literature suggest far less interest on the part of Caucasian adopters in older children of color, particularly children with histories of abuse and neglect and foster care placement. Studies that examine parental preferences related to race, disability status, and age are somewhat dated but suggest that adoptive families, in general, do not express an interest in adopting older children, children with disabilities, or children of African American heritage [Meezan et al. 1978; Kossoudji 1989]. While it is possible that attitudes among prospective adopters have changed, neither the research nor recent statistics suggest a greater demand by Caucasian families for African American children in general nor for older children [Courtney 1997].

In addition to the supply-related factors associated with the age and ethnicity of children in care is the fact that, increasingly, children in the foster care system for whom adoption is the permanency plan have "special needs." Although states vary in their definitions of "special needs," most states base the determination on physical, emotional and mental disability; older age of the child; racial minority status, usually in conjunction with older age; and being part of a sibling group [Sedlak & Broadhurst 1992]. The proportion of children in foster care with special needs who are adopted has risen significantly over the past two decades. In FY 1984, 47% of these children were determined to have special needs; by FY 1990, the proportion had risen to almost three-quarters (72%); and by FY 1998, 86% of the children had special needs [Tatara 1993; U.S. Department of Health & Human Services 2000]. Of this group of children determined to have "special needs," a substantial percentage have significant health problems. Studies have found that as many as 60% of children in foster care have mental health problems in the moderate to severe range, and approximately 40% suffer from physical health problems [Halfon et al. 1994]. A study of children under three years of age who entered foster care in Los Angeles County, New York City, and Philadelphia in 1986 or 1991 found that more than four-fifths of the children had at least one serious health problem [U.S. General Accounting Office 1994].

Compromised health and developmental status—characteristics of many children in foster care waiting for adoptive families—have an impact on the supply of adoptive families in much the same way as age. Generally, prospective adoptive parents seek to adopt healthy children and may not consider themselves prepared to adopt a child with special health, mental health, or developmental needs. But do such generalities capture the full range of prospective adoptive parents for children in care? Do age and the health and developmental status of children waiting in foster care work, in reality, against the recruitment of well-prepared, loving families for these children? Or are certain assumptions about the adoptability of these children at work, creating artificial barriers to recruitment?

The Current Supply

Currently, children in foster care are adopted by three major types of families: former foster parents, relatives, and families unrelated to them. The extent to which each of these groups adopts children in foster care has changed over time. In FY 1990, a little less than half of the children in foster care freed for adoption were adopted by former foster parents (47%), a small percentage were adopted by relatives (7%), and a large percentage were adopted by people unrelated to them (42%) [Tatara 1993]. By FY 1998, there was a significant shift in the demographics of adoptive families for this group of children. A significantly larger percentage of children were adopted by unrelated foster parents (65%); relatives (other than step parents) comprised a somewhat larger group of adopters (15%); and there had been a marked decline in the proportion of adoptions of these children by non-relatives (20%) [Department of Health & Human Services 2000]. These trends raise significant issues related to the nature of the current supply of families and the challenges inherent in expanding the pool of adoptive families to meet the growing demand.

Adoption by Former Foster Parents. Although nationally about three-fifths of all special needs adoptions are by foster parents, the proportion is even higher in some states, with some communities reporting that 80% to 90% of children are adopted by foster parents [McKenzie 1993]. The majority of foster parents adopt children who were previously placed with them [U.S. Department of Health and Human Services 1992], and experts predict, based on current trends, that the percentage of foster parents who adopt the children for whom they are already caring will continue to rise [McKenzie 1993]. Although this trend might suggest a ready pool of prospective adoptive parents for children in foster care, the actual size of this population of prospective adoptive parents has decreased both in absolute numbers and in relation to the increased demand.

The total number of foster parents has significantly declined since the 1980s as, simultaneously, the number of children in foster care has risen. It is estimated that the number of foster parents who are unrelated to the children for whom they are caring decreased from approximately 147,000 in 1984 to 100,000 in 1990 [Chamberlain, Moreland & Reid 1992], although two child welfare researchers indicate that the number recently increased slightly once again [Petit & Curtis 1997]. The recruitment of new foster parents and the retention of current foster parents have presented challenges. In addition to the difficulties associated with recruiting new foster families, one expert estimates that the annual attrition rate for approved foster families is as high as 50% annually in some states [Terpstra 2000]. Many experts predict that a shortage in the number of foster homes, in light of the growing number of children in care needing foster parents, will persist and the total number of foster parents will continue to decline [HHS 1992].

Efforts to increase the number of foster parents generally have not been successful. Even states that have undertaken intensive, multimillion dollar efforts to recruit more foster parents find that they currently have even fewer foster parents than before their recruitment campaigns began [Grunwald 1997]. This trend may translate into the availability of fewer foster parents for increasing numbers of children—either to provide short-term foster care or to offer the permanency of adoption. If, as many experts predict, this population of prospective adoptive parents cannot be viewed as the ongoing solution to the supply-side needs in special needs adoption, the question becomes to what extent other adoptive family resources can be pursued.

Adoption by Relatives. An alternative source of adoptive families is the extended family networks of the children themselves. For children in foster care needing adoption, relatives generally have adopted through two routes. Some serve as children's foster parents and then adopt; others offer to adopt their relative-children initially placed with unrelated foster parents once the decision to pursue adoption is made. It is estimated that approximately 30% of the children in foster care are placed with related foster parents, with considerably higher percentages in certain urban areas [Child Welfare League of America 1994]. Many of these relatives are willing to adopt, but others may feel that they are not able to meet the children's longer-term needs [McKenzie 1993]. At the same time, the literature suggests that many family members who serve as foster parentsVoften grandmothers—have misgivings about formal adoption because of their own age or health status; concerns that adoption evidences disrespect for the child's relationship to the birth parent; and financial considerations related to the ongoing care of children on their limited incomes [Testa et al. 1996].

Alternatively, extended family members may adopt their young relatives whose stays with unrelated foster parents have not led to reunification with their birth families as may have been originally contemplated [McKenzie 1993]. The extent to which this group of relatives could become an adoptive family resource for children in foster care warrants closer scrutiny. Their under-utilization as adoptive families may be related to concerns similar to those articulated by relative foster parents or, alternatively, may reflect a lack of interest on the part of child welfare systems in exploring the availability of such families, particularly when they reside in counties or states other than the child's place of residence.

Recent policy changes seem to suggest greater support for larger numbers of relative adoptions. The data suggest, at least at this point, that adoption by relatives has increased—both among those who initially provide foster care and those who step forward when the child welfare agency determines that reunification with birth parents will not be pursued [U.S. Department of Health & Human Services 1999]. The Personal Responsibility and Work Opportunities Reconciliation Act of 1996 requires that the child welfare agency with custody give preferential consideration to adult relatives when determining out-of-home care for a child [Courtney 1999]. ASFA similarly acknowledges the role of kin in caring for their relative children [42 U.S.C. § 675(e)(4)(E)], although some view ASFA requirements related to criminal background checks as creating barriers to adoption for many families of color as a result of criminal justice system practices in relation to African American men [Howe 2000]. Policy has not addressed some of the key issues raised by the fact that the adoption of related children is primarily by families with lower incomes [see Mosher & Bachrach 1996]. The financial impact of adoption on lower-income families including relatives—particularly in relation to the availability of adoption assistance for their relative children— is a critical market force issue that requires attention and will be discussed later in this book.

    Adoption by Unrelated Families. An alternative group of prospective adopters is comprised of families who are unrelated to the child whom they adopt and who have not served as foster parents for these or other children. As the FY 1990 and FY 1998 data reflect, a declining percentage of adoptions of children in foster care is by unrelated families. Some experts voice concern that adoption of children in foster care by unrelated families will continue to decline [McKenzie 1993]. Data show that overall, adoptions of unrelated children are most commonly by childless women, women with fecundity impairments, Caucasian women, and those with higher levels of income and education [Mosher & Bachrach 1996], and these groups historically have adopted healthy infants, not children in foster care. Questions remain as to whether this group of adults might be recruited as adoptive families for children in care. Is it correct to assume, as do some adoption professionals, that this group of potential adopters simply has no interest in adopting children with special needs? Or, is there a potential interest among this group of prospective adoptive parents that could be tapped more effectively?

    At the same time, reports from the field indicate that the adults who adopt children who are in foster care, particularly children with special needs, tend to have different demographic and socioeconomic characteristics than the population of adopters described by Mosher and Bachrach [1996] in their research. Holtan [1999] notes that nonrelated families who adopt older children with special needs tend to be of lower to middle income, high school graduates or holding some college-level education, and single or married with biological children. Questions also arise as to how this population of adoptive families could be further expanded, particularly given the limited financial resources that these families often have available to them.

Expanding the Pool of Adoptive Families

A critical aspect of the supply-side challenges associated with special needs adoption is the expansion of the pool of adoptive families. The current diversity of families in this country suggests a social environment that supports a broad view of family and, consequently, a more inclusive view as to who may adopt that extends beyond the traditional profile of Caucasian, married, and middle to upper income couples. The field of special needs adoption already has broadened its acceptance of prospective adoptive parents in relation to certain demographic variables— specifically, nonmarital status and to a lesser, but growing degree, sexual orientation. A range of issues remains as to the extent to which the field has extended and could further develop recruitment efforts designed to reach communities of color.

Paralleling the increase in the number of single individuals who achieve parenthood through biological procreation [United States Bureau of the Census 1994; Vobejda 1996] has been the significant growth in the number of single-parent adoptions over the past decade. Single parents now represent an important family resource for waiting children in foster care and currently constitute one-quarter or more of the adopters of children with special needs [Shireman 1995], a figure that compares to only 2.5% in 1975 [Meezan 1980]. State-based studies and national data validate the growth in single parent adoptions. In Oregon, for example, 5% of all placements made by the Children's Services Division in 1989 were with single parents; by 1991, the figure had risen to 12% [Shireman 1995]. Avery and Mont [1994] found an even higher proportion of single adopters in their study of adoptive families in New York State: one-half of families adopting children with special needs were single-parent families. In his review of twelve studies of family composition in special needs adoption, Groze [1991] found varying proportions of single-parent adopters, ranging from a low of .5% in a study conducted in 1970 to a high of 34% in a study conducted in 1984. Data from the U.S. Children's Bureau indicate that in FY 1998, almost one-third (31%) of all children adopted from foster care were adopted by single women and 2% by single men [Maza 1999].

There also has been somewhat greater flexibility in special needs adoption in relation to the sexual orientation of prospective adoptive parents. Although data do not exist to demonstrate the extent to which gay and lesbian individuals have adopted children from foster care, some suggest that in certain areas of the country, the population of adoptive parents has been expanded through greater acceptance of gay and lesbian adoptive parents [Tasker & Golombok 1997]. In California and New York, for example, it is illegal to reject a prospective adoptive parent solely on the basis of sexual orientation [Tasker & Golombok 1997]. Nonetheless, even in those jurisdictions, prospective adopters may be rejected on other bases [Martin 1993]. In some states, there continue to be express prohibitions on adoption by gays and lesbians through legislation or administrative policy [Ricketts & Achtenberg 1990], and other states are currently considering legislative or administrative policies to effect the same result [Rivera 1999]. Under these circumstances, it is not unusual to find that adoptive parents choose to keep their sexual orientation "invisible" as to licensing authorities or until adoptions are finalized [Parks 1998, p. 381].

While there is consensus that the "the system needs good adoptive parents" [Crawford 1999, p. 276], the debate continues as to whether that need is one that exists "regardless of sexual orientation" [Crawford 1999, p. 276] or is a need that must be met on the basis of traditional principles that retain marriage in "its special status as the proper place for rearing children" [Walliser 1997, interview with Steve Schwalm of the Family Research Council]. As society's definition of family has expanded and a broad range of nontraditional families has come to characterize U.S. society [Shapiro & Schultz 1985/1986], it may be that gay men and lesbians will enjoy greater acceptance as parents and be seen as important resources for waiting children in foster care. The current "volatile and ongoing battle of value judgments and civil rights," however, may be, as Crawford [1999, p. 271] notes, "draining the life—the spirit, the goodness, the energy, and the genuineness—from our pool of prospective parents whom we so desperately need."

Another critical issue in the expansion of the supply of adoptive parents for children in foster care relates to the racial and cultural backgrounds of prospective adoptive parents. As virtually every commentator on the foster care system has noted, children of color are overrepresented in the foster care population as a whole, and they wait longer than Caucasian children for adoption, if and when it is decided that adoption planning and services are appropriate for them [Lawrence-Webb 1997; Brown & Bailey-Etta 1997; McKenzie 1993]. Studies have shown that African American children are more than twice as likely to remain in foster care as to be adopted, compared to Caucasian children who are about twice as likely to be adopted as to remain in care [Barth 1997]. Latino children are about equally likely to remain in foster ca're as to be adopted [Barth 1997].

In response to concerns about the large number of children of color waiting for adoptive families for lengthy periods of time, federal law was changed in 1994 and then again in 1996 to facilitate the adoption of waiting children in care along transracial lines. Underlying the legislation—the Multi-Ethnic Placement Act of 1994 [P.L. 103-382] and the Inter-Ethnic Placement Act of 1996 [P.L. 104-188] was the belief that children of color, in general, and African American children, in particular, were not being adopted because of race-based decision-making in adoptive placements [McRoy et al. 1997]. The expectation underlying this policy was that by facilitating adoption by Caucasian families, larger numbers of children of color in foster care would move into adoption in a more timely manner.

Because there is no definitive source of data on a national basis regarding transracial adoptions of children with special needs, no data exist to establish the extent to which these adoptions occurred or were prohibited in the past. Most analyses suggest that relatively few transracial adoptions have taken place over the past two decades. A Child Welfare League of America [1995] survey of 22 states, for example, found that 4% of all adoptions of children in foster care in 1993 were transracial, and Stolley [1993] reported that only about 1% of all adoptions involved adoptions of African American children by Caucasian parents. Avery and Mont [1994] found in their New York State study that approximately 11% of adoptions among a sample of 258 families were transracial. The researchers reported that in most instances, Caucasian parents adopted African American children [10.68%]. Only in a very small number of adoptions [.83% or 3 cases] did African American parents adopt a Caucasian child [1994]. A relationship between these low rates of transracial adoption and the lengthy waits for adoption experienced by children of color in foster care has not been demonstrated.

Likewise, it is not clear whether changes in federal law that promote transracial adoption will positively impact the supply of adoptive families for children in foster care. Those who support transracial adoption maintain that recent policy changes that preclude consideration of race in adoptive placements will facilitate the adoption of children of color by Caucasian families, resulting in a large pool of these families coming forward to adopt [Bartholet 1993]. This position largely has been supported by anecdotal accounts and not by data that demonstrate that Caucasian families, in significant numbers, have sought and been deprived of the opportunity to adopt African American and other children of color with special needs. There appears to be no research that addresses the extent to which Caucasian families seek to adopt children of color, particularly children in foster care;

the extent to which such families have been screened out as prospective adoptive families on the basis of race; or the extent to which these families have sought alternate forms of adoption, such as international adoption, because of rejection by the public child welfare agencies system. Nonetheless, these arguments have been advanced in an attempt to explain the lengthy waits of children of color in foster care and to make the case that the needed supply of adoptive families for these children can be met readily through transracial adoptions.

Those who oppose the facilitation of transracial adoption contend that prospective African American and other adoptive families of color are available for waiting children in foster care, but barriers within the child welfare system have made it difficult for these families to adopt [Neal 1996]. Although many experts have pointed to the failure of the child welfare system itself to effectively reach prospective adoptive families of color [McRoy et al. 1997; McKenzie 1993], including the disproportionate screening out of prospective African American families [Hill 1993; Howe 2000], the adoption literature commonly assumes that African American and other adults of color lack interest in the formal adoption of children in foster care [National Committee for Adoption 1989]. There has been little empirical study of the actual extent to which members of communities of color, including African American communities, are willing to pursue formal adoption [Kalmuss 1992], although there are reported surveys that reflect that significant numbers of African American heads of household are interested in formally adopting [Hill 1993].

Specifically with regard to prospective adoptive families within the African American community, Kalmuss [1992] argues that there are significant potential resources among African American couples with fertility problems and also among single African American adults who want a child, do not anticipate marrying, and, with respect to African American women, do not wish to have a non-marital birth. Kupenda [1996/1997, pp. 708–709] agrees, noting that the number of single, African American women who desire children in the context of traditional nuclear families may be far greater than "like-minded single black men" and that many of these women, moreover, may "legitimately prefer to remain single" while desiring to be a parent. Adding to the groups identified by Kalmuss, Kupenda recommends an additional model for African American adoptions which would allow "two single people who each qualify to adopt as a single person but choose to adopt together as co-parents" [1996/1997, p. 705]. She argues that this type of adoptive family structure may "actually be the natural and the traditional model for African Americans" and may respond better to the current realities facing African American children who need families and African American adults who wish to parent [Kupenda 1996/1997, p. 711].

Unanswered questions remain about the knowledge and attitudes about adoption held by adults of color, their perceptions of the adoption system's degree of openness to them and their perceptions of the level of support in their own communities for adults who adopt unrelated children [Kalmuss 1992]. Nonetheless, a number of adoption recruitment programs targeting communities of color have been successful in reaching prospective adoptive families of color [McRoy et al. 1997], including, as one example, the Kentucky One Church One Child Program, which increased the adoptions of African American children by 100% through targeted recruitment of African American families [Black Adoption Project 1992]. These outcomes suggest that it would be inaccurate to assume that adults of color have little interest in the adoption of children in foster care.

Federal law recognizes the need to actively recruit adoptive families for children in foster care who will not return to their birth families. In the Multi-Ethnic Placement Act of 1994 (MEPA), Congress expressly found that:

> active, creative and diligent efforts are needed to recruit foster and adoptive parents of every race, ethnicity, and culture in order to facilitate the placement of children in foster and adoptive homes which will best meet each child's needs [P.L. 103-382, §651(a)(5)].

To that end, the law requires that child welfare agencies engage in "diligent recruitment of potential foster and adoptive families that reflect the ethnic and racial diversity of children in the State for whom foster and adoptive homes are needed" [§554(3)]. Subsequent amendments in 1996 changed other aspects of the 1994 law, but the recruitment mandate remained intact. In a similar vein, the Adoption and Safe Families Act of 1997 (ASFA) mandated specific efforts on the part of child welfare agencies to recruit families for children in foster care for whom "the permanency plan is adoption or placement in another foster home" with requirements that child welfare agencies document the steps made to recruit families for such children and include within these steps "at minimum ... child specific recruitment efforts" [42 U.S.C. §675(1)(E)].

Despite the recognition of the overriding importance of adoptive family recruitment for waiting children in foster care, neither MEPA nor ASFA allocated resources at any level for general or child specific recruitment activities. State and county child welfare agencies are, presumably, expected to mount diligent recruitment efforts for the growing number of children freed for adoption with existing fiscal and staff resources. This expectation raises important issues: To what extent can a mandate of "diligent recruitment" that takes into account the "ethnic and racial diversity of children" in care be implemented without a commitment of resources? Does the absence of additional resources reflect an assessment of the actual importance of these activities? Of these children? Of outreach to the ethnic and racial communities from which these children come?

The Ethical Issues Regarding Supply and Demand

There are a number of questions with ethical implications regarding the growing demand for adoption services by children in foster care and the limited supply of adoptive families for these children. Specifically:

- To what extent is poverty driving the need for adoption by this group of children? Is the combined effect of federal policy in the form of welfare reform (The Personal Responsibility and Work Opportunity Reconciliation Act) and adoption reform (The Adoption and Safe Families Act) principally one of subjecting poor parents—as opposed to unfit parents—to termination of parental rights? Do these policies, as argued by Howe [2000], reflect, in essence, "a continuing deep seated and judgmental devaluing of the families from which these children come"?

• What will be the effect on children of greater use of involuntary termination of parental rights? Will compliance with federal mandates to file petitions to terminate parental rights result in a growing, and possibly unmanageably large, population children who are "waiting" for adoptive families?

• Has adequate attention been given to the "match" between the characteristics of waiting children and the general interests of adults who seek to adopt? Is the apparent "mis-match"—in relation to a combination of waiting children's age, ethnicity, and health status and the apparent preferences of many prospective adoptive parents—an insurmountable barrier or a challenge which can be met?

• What is the level of commitment to expanding the supply of adoptive parents for children in foster care?

• Are legislative mandates to recruit and philosophical statements related to the importance of adoptive families for children in foster care meaningful in the absence of resources to implement such efforts?

• To what extent should efforts be made to promote adoption by foster parents and children's relatives? To what extent should adoption by unrelated families be promoted? And, of this pool of prospective adoptive parents, are certain sectors considered more appropriate than others and on what basis?

The Role of Money in Special Needs Adoption: Subsidy and Postadoption Services

Money, as in the case of infant and international adoption, plays a major role in the adoption of children in foster care. Two key issues affect this group of children and their adoptive families: (1) access to and the level of available subsidies for children with special needs who are adopted from foster care; and (2) the extent to which resources are available to develop and sustain post-adoption services and supports for these children and their families.

Subsidy as a Support for Adopted Children with Special Needs

Because of the physical, mental health, and developmental needs of many children in foster care, the economic issues confronting their adoptions principally relate to financial support for families and children after adoptive placements and the finalization of adoptions [Jacoby 1999]. Fees and expenses for adoptions arranged by public agencies typically range from zero to only a nominal amount [Jacoby 1999], and consequently, significant up-front adoption-related expenses, to which the federal tax credit responds, are not the predominant issue for these families. Instead, the monetary issue relates to adopted children's longer-term needs, which may require specialized services and place ongoing financial demands on their adoptive families.

When children in foster care who will be placed with adoptive families are determined to have "special needs," they are eligible for adoption subsidies, also known as adoption assistance. The Adoption Assistance and Child Welfare Act of 1980 [P.L. 96-272] established the federal adoption assistance program for children in foster care with special needs and authorized the use of federal funds to pay a significant portion of the adoption subsidies for children who qualify for federally-funded foster care (under Title IV-E of the Social Security Act) or the federal Supplemental Security Income (SSI) program (a program for low income children with disabilities). In addition to the federally-funded subsidy program, many states offer state-funded subsidy benefits for adopted children with special needs who do not qualify for the federally funded program, although the eligibility criteria and level of benefits vary significantly from one state to another. Adoption subsidies are essentially small monthly stipends, and in the federally funded program, they typically range from $300 to $500 per child [Katz 1999]. The level of a child's adoption subsidy may not exceed the level of monthly foster care payment that the state would have made on behalf of the child had she remained in family foster care [Oppenheim et al. 1999].

Although the monthly amount of any individual subsidy is quite modest, subsidies are seen as playing a vital role in special needs adoption, both because of the financial assistance they provide to adoptive families and because subsidies carry with them health care coverage for the child, either through Medicaid or another health insurance program. Oppenheim and colleagues [1999, p. 9-3] write:

> One factor that inhibits the adoption of children with special needs is the cost of caring for them. This financial burden often makes it impossible for a family or a single person with low or moderate income to consider adopting a child with special needs. However, the adoption assistance programs provided by the state and federal government have made it possible for many families and single persons to adopt children who otherwise would languish in foster care.

Similarly, Katz [1999, p. A27] notes that adoption subsidies paid to the adoptive parents of children with special needs are:

> necessary, if no other reason than to avoid creating a negative financial incentive for foster families to adopt children in their care. Given the supply and demand economics of adoption, people who adopt children from foster care are overwhelmingly of modest means. The adoption subsidy is critical in allowing them to be able to adopt.

These assessments of the critical role of subsidy in special needs adoption are shared by a number of researchers who have

evaluated the role of subsidy in promoting and sustaining the
adoptions of children with special needs [Barth & Berry 1988;
Gilles 1995; Sedlak & Broadhurst 1992]. Research has found, for
example, that subsidy decreases the average waiting time of
children in foster care for adoptive families and facilitates the
adoptions of children whose first adoptive placements disrupted
[Sedlak & Broadhurst 1992]. Nonetheless, issues remain regarding
the extent to which current subsidy programs and policies respond appropriately to the needs of children who move from
foster care to adoption and the needs of their adoptive families.

Access to subsidy. A number of studies have demonstrated
that federally-funded adoption assistance has not consistently been
made available to all children who are eligible for the program.
Although the number of children who receive adoption assistance
has grown substantially since the program was established in 1980
[North American Council on Adoptable Children 1996], many children with special needs who are eligible for subsidy do not receive
this support. In a multistate study of adoption assistance programs,
Gilles [1995] found that 13% of the adoptive parents of children with
special needs were not notified of the adoption assistance program,
and one-fifth of children with special needs were placed without
monthly subsidy payments. Sedlak and Broadhurst [1992], in their
study of 40,700 children adopted between 1983 and 1987, determined that 84% of the children had one or more characteristics
meeting their state's definition of "special needs," but only 63% of
the children were adopted with a subsidy. Barth and Berry [1988]
found that although prohibited by federal law, many programs
determined children's eligibility for subsidy based on the adoptive
family's income. In their study of adoptions of children with special
needs that did not include a subsidy, they found that in over 50% of
the cases, the agency decided not to provide the child with a subsidy
because of the adoptive family's level of income [Barth & Berry 1988].

Despite the permanency goals of ASFA and the range of
special needs of the majority of children in foster care who await
adoptive families, there are significant income-based barriers to
establishing children's eligibility for subsidy. Children with special needs are eligible for federally funded adoption assistance

only if they were previously eligible for foster care under Title IV-E of the Social Security Act—which is tied to eligibility for the former AFDC program—or are eligible for the Supplemental Security Income (SSI) program at the time of adoption. With "welfare reform," it has become more complicated to establish eligibility for Title IV-E foster care. The rules implementing welfare reform state that the financial eligibility criteria, which serve as the basis for adoption subsidies, is tied to the AFDC program abolished in 1996. Children, consequently, may qualify for adoption subsidies if they meet eligibility rules that existed at a point in the past (July 16, 1996) for a program (AFDC) that no longer exists. The linkage between adoption assistance eligibility (through Title IV-E) and AFDC eligibility has been identified as one of the major impediments to children's ability to access adoption subsidies [Gilles 1995].

Efforts have been made, at the federal level, to "de-link" eligibility for adoption assistance—the federal subsidy program—from eligibility for the former AFDC program. This legislation has not garnered significant political support, in large measure because of concerns that too many children would qualify for subsidy and an expanded subsidy program would be prohibitively expensive. Although an increase in the number of subsidized adoptions would generate an increase in subsidy budgets on a point-in-time basis, subsidy payments over time are likely to be less expensive than continued foster care. Adoption subsidies are, on average, less than foster care payments in absolute terms and do not incorporate the relatively high administrative costs of the foster care program [Weidermeier-Bower 1997]. Nonetheless, fiscal concerns have posed barriers to "de-linking" efforts. By contrast, legislative efforts to increase the tax credit for adoption—which does not benefit families who adopt children with special needs but instead subsidizes higher cost adoptions by higher-income families—has not generated an equivalent level of fiscal concern.

Adding to the barriers posed by the linkage of AFDC and adoption subsidy are the changes in the SSI program that have significantly limited the number of children with disabilities who are eligible for benefits. Because of program eligibility changes, many children who may have had the SSI connection needed to qualify for adoption assistance in the past no longer qualify for SSI. With changes in the eligibility criteria under both Title IV-E and SSI, key resources supporting the adoption of children with special needs—the subsidies themselves and the publicly funded health care coverage (through Medicaid or an equivalent program) that accompanies subsidy—may not be available to many children whose adoptions depend on these ongoing supports. It is not unreasonable to anticipate that barriers to subsidy and health insurance support could affect the ability of many prospective adoptive families of moderate means to assume full responsibility for children with special needs [Oppenheim et al. 1999].

It is important to note that ASFA addressed two issues related to access, which promote some children's continued support following adoption. Under ASFA, children who receive adoption subsidies but whose adoptions disrupt before finalization must retain their eligibility for subsidy. Additionally, children with special needs who are not eligible for a federally-funded subsidy and who receive a state-funded adoption subsidy must be provided with health care coverage at a level equivalent to the state's Medicaid coverage. These provisions clearly provide support for some proportion of children deemed eligible for subsidy. They fall short, however, of achieving broader goals of equitable subsidy access for children with special needs.

Level of subsidy. When children are determined to be eligible for and receive federally-funded adoption subsidies, the level of subsidy may not exceed the foster care maintenance rate [Oppenheim et al. 1999]. Weidermeier-Bower [1997] found in her analysis of subsidy levels and foster care maintenance rates for children at different ages that the monthly adoption subsidy was, on average, consistently lower than the foster care rate for all age groups of children. She found that compared to the average foster care payment, the average subsidy was $11 less per month for children at age 2 ($342 compared to $353); $8 less per month for children at age 9 ($363 compared to $371); and $10 less per month for children at age 16 ($419 compared to $ 429). Although subsidy programs were not designed to meet the full cost of care of a child with special needs [Sullivan 2000], it is also the case that children with greater needs do not have higher subsidies [Barth & Berry 1988].

The current modest level of subsidy may be reduced to even lower levels as economic considerations impact the program. The Texas Department of Protective and Regulatory Services, for example, announced that effective December 1, 1999, children with special needs adopted from foster care would be eligible for adoption subsidy at a level no higher than the basic foster care rate [Kroll 1999b]. Under this policy, if a child had received a specialized foster care rate while in care because of intensive physical, mental health or developmental needs, she would, at the time of adoption, qualify for an adoption subsidy only at the lower, basic foster care rate [Kroll 1999b]. Although it may affect only a limited number of families, Kroll [1999b, p. 1] notes that this policy change:

> fails . . . to allow for cases in which would-be adopters require more support due to children's exceptional needs. In those situations, the policy may discourage families from pursuing adoption.

The rationale behind such a policy change appears to be the impact on adoption assistance budgets as the number of adoptions of subsidy-eligible children with special needs continues to grow. The North American Council on Adoptable Children [Kroll 1999b] estimates that by 2001, the portion of adoption subsidy payments paid by the federal government will exceed $1 billion. Increases in spending at the state level are likely to parallel the increases at the federal level, potentially leading to decisions to limit adoption assistance levels for all children, including those with intensive needs [Kroll 1999b]. Nonetheless, is a reduction in benefits for families who adopt children with special needs the answer to increased demands on adoption subsidy budgets? Kroll [1999b, p. 2] argues that the solution lies elsewhere:

And as we work to increase the number of children in foster care who find permanence, states should make concerted efforts to shore up the resources that can keep children safe and secure in their new families. States that cut support for adoptive families may soon find that fewer and fewer families are stepping forward to provide permanence for waiting children.

Ethical Considerations related to Subsidy. The current adoption subsidy program raises a number of questions with ethical implications. Specifically, these questions focus on:

- The practice of some states in failing to inform adoptive parents of the availability of subsidy for eligible children with special needs whom they wish to adopt;

- The failure at the policy level to implement an accessible and equitable program of subsidy for children with special needs adopted from foster care, particularly given the continuing linkage of eligibility for adoption subsidy with the defunct AFDC program and with the constricted SSI program; and

- The maintenance of adoption subsidies at low and, in some programs, even lower levels of support.

The most reasonable explanation underlying these practices is an economic one, predominated by considerations related to limited resources and a desire to save public dollars through controls on the number of children with special needs who qualify for subsidy and the level of subsidy received by qualifying children. It is unlikely that these practices or policies are based on beliefs that children with special needs adopted from foster care do not actually need services or support as a result of their physical, mental health, or developmental status, or that the families who adopt these children are doing so simply to generate additional income for themselves. Nonetheless, what do policies and practices designed to constrain subsidy costs convey about assumptions regarding children in foster care and the families who adopt them? Are children adopted from foster care "worth" a financial investment to enable them to have permanent families? Are their adoptive families considered as deserving of financial support as are more affluent families, including those who benefit from the adoption tax credit? Are more affluent families and the infants they adopt seen as "better" in some sense and, therefore, more deserving of support than more moderate income families and the older and/or physically, mentally, or developmentally compromised children they adopt?

Financial Support for Postadoption Services

The second fiscal issue that impacts the adoption of children in foster care is the extent to which postadoption services are available for children adopted from foster care and for their adoptive families. A significant percentage of children in foster care have substantial needs that require ongoing medical, mental health, and developmental services [Halfon et al. 1994]. Given their histories of abuse and neglect, their transitions into new adoptive families often present special challenges. Assuming success in locating prospective adoptive families, the question becomes whether systems are in place to ensure the stability of these families following adoptive placements and, particularly, after adoptions are finalized.

Practitioners have pointed consistently to the availability of postadoption support and services as critical to the availability and stability of adoptive families for children in foster care [Voice for Adoption 1997]. Although there is no reported research on the relationship between the availability of postadoption services and the recruitment of adoptive families for children with special needs, it is reasonable to assume that families would be more likely to adopt children with physical or mental health problems or significant developmental delays if there is assurance of support after placement and finalization [Freundlich 1997]. An understanding that postadoption services will be readily available—whether in connection with subsidy or on an as-needed basis—may provide families with the confidence they need to move forward with the decision to adopt.

Similarly, the availability of postadoption services is likely to enhance adoptive family stability. Postadoption support and services have been shown to strengthen adoptive families of children with special needs and prevent adoption disruption. Adoption disruption is associated with older age at the time of adoptive placement [Barth et al. 1986] and with histories of abuse, severe neglect, and multiple foster care placements [Sullivan 1999], factors involved in the adoptive placements of many children with special needs. A number of studies have correlated adoption disruption with the absence of effective family support services and children's developmental and emotional disabilities [Barth et al. 1986; Groze 1985; Pearlman-Smith 1989; Rosenthal et al. 1988].

Postadoption services, however, often are not available to adoptive families. Agency resources often are devoted principally to providing preadoption services for waiting children [Marcenko & Smith 1991], and, consequently, fewer than one-third of the states have a formal program of services after legalization of children's adoptions [Barth 1997]. Studies of adoptive families' needs for and use of postadoption services suggest that there is a considerable gap between need and service availability. Nelson [1985], in her study of the availability of formal and informal networks of services, found that adoptive families often had difficulty obtaining many of the services they needed and that when services were available, families often found them to be unsatisfactory. Marcenko and Smith [1991] similarly found that adoptive families lacked access to basic family support services such as respite care and support groups. Consistent with the overall economic demographics of families who adopt children from foster care, the families they studied were of modest means, with the "higher income" families in an annual income range of $35,000 to $40,000. Research suggests that needs for postadoption services are associated, to some degree, with families' economic resources. Meaker [1989], for example, found that services were most often needed by families facing financial pressures as a result of their children exhibiting higher levels of problems than had been anticipated.

Watson [1992, p. 11] has highlighted the reality that "post-legal adoption services cost money," and urges that the case for post-adoption services be made on fiscal grounds that highlight earlier investments. He [1999, p. 12] writes:

> A sound argument can be made that the families who have adopted special-needs children are by definition especially vulnerable to dissolution. Since the states have already invested resources in putting such families together, to not invest additional funds to keep those families together would seem foolish.

This vision of the long-term value of postadoption services may provide a powerful justification for these services. Policy and practice, however, have not viewed postadoption services as essential to protecting existing investments in children's well-being. The Adoption and Safe Families Act, for example—despite its emphasis on increasing the use of adoption as a permanency option for children in foster care—did not allocate resources for postadoption services. The incentive structure of ASFA rewards states for increased numbers of adoptions, but offers no corresponding incentive to states to provide services to promote the stability of adoptions once they are finalized. At the state level, it is likely that budgets for post-adoption services will be subjected to the same scrutiny as subsidy budgets and that the fiscal resources allocated to post-adoption services will continue to be limited. These realities raise important issues with ethical implications:

- To what extent are the needs of adoptive families of children with special needs given priority—particularly in allocating sufficient resources to programs to support them? Is the failure to develop and fully support adoptive families a case of public neglect?

- Does the absence of postadoption services and support indicate a philosophy that these families, having adopted children with special needs, are and should be "on their own"?

- Will attention be given to these issues only in the face of increased numbers of adoption disruptions that traumatize children and families and, from a systems perspective, cost public agencies more money in foster care services and "re-placement" of children with new adoptive families?

Summary

The market forces impacting the adoption of children in foster care are no less significant than the forces that affect infant and international adoption. Money, power, and accountability are critical dynamics in a system in which the growing demand for adoption planning and services has clearly exceeded the supply of adoptive families. The level of need for adoption planning and services has been associated with poverty, and that relationship is likely to continue to characterize foster care entry, termination of parental rights, and adoption services as the effects of welfare reform and adoption reform become more evident. At the same time, child welfare systems face critical challenges in ensuring that children with adoption as their permanency plan are placed with well-prepared and well-supported families. The imbalance between the current and projected levels of demand and the current supply of adoptive families raises a key issue related to outcomes for children who remain in foster care waiting for adoptive families. The extent to which resources are committed to expanding the pool of adoptive families is a critical measurement of society's assessment of the "worth"of these children.

Money, as in infant and international adoption, exerts a significant force in the adoption of children in foster care. Families who adopt children with special needs from foster care face few financial barriers to the adoption process, but often confront significant financial demands in meeting the ongoing physical, mental health, and developmental needs of their adopted children. Current subsidy policy and practice raise a host of questions, with ethical implications involving equitable access to financial assistance and health care, and fairness in the level of support that is provided in relation to intensity of need. There are, likewise, important issues with ethical implications—in terms of the value placed on these children and families—in the provision of postadoption services.

Part IV

The Role of Marketing in Adoption

A final area for consideration in relation to the market forces that characterize adoption practice is the range of activities that fall, to a greater or lesser degree, within the rubric of "marketing." Each of these activities raises issues regarding adoption as a service for children, birth parents, and adoptive parents. Should prospective adoptive parents "market" themselves? Is it appropriate to "market" children who are available for adoption? To what extent is marketing by adoption agencies, adoption attorneys, and facilitators acceptable advertising? Is there a point at which these activities cross the boundary into unacceptable or questionable practice? In this section, marketing and the ethical issues it raises are explored in three contexts: (1) marketing by prospective adoptive parents in an effort to "find a baby"; (2) marketing of children for purposes of adoption; and (3) marketing by adoption service providers to attract business.

Marketing by Prospective Adoptive Parents

Increasingly, prospective adoptive parents undertake activities to make their interest in adoption known to birth parents who may be considering placing their infants for adoption. More than a decade ago, the first classified notices appeared in newspapers in which prospective adoptive parents sought to connect with birth parents seeking families for their infants. In contrast to earlier notices such as "PREGNANT? Young couple wishes to adopt baby. Call Mary at . . ." in local newspapers, personal advertisements now run in national newspapers such as *USA Today* and other publications, and appear on the Internet. These notices often include descriptive information about the prospective adoptive parents and frequently refer to their financial ability to provide extremely well for a child whom they wish to adopt. One recent notice [*USA Today* 1999], for example, indicated that the prospective adoptive family would "shower your child with love, laughter, and every opportunity for a promising future." Other notices focus on the stability of the adoptive couple ("Highschool sweethearts...Christian faith important" or "Stay home mom"); their lovely houses ("great home" or "beautiful home"); and their ability to treat a child to wonderful experiences ("fun times and vacations" or "fun summers at the lake") [www.adopting.org 1999].

Anecdotal reports of successful connections between prospective adoptive parents and birth parents suggest that such techniques can lead to positive outcomes for the adults involved and the children placed by their birth families with new adoptive families. Such advertising, however, also raises concerns about what it may convey about adoption itself and about the qualities to be valued in prospective adoptive parents. Gritter [1999, p. 9] maintains that such personal advertising, which he views as a cornerstone of the commercial approach to adoption, positions prospective adoptive parents as "products in need of clever packaging."

While some may view personal advertising by prospective adoptive parents as "intrinsically tacky," Gritter observes that more importantly, such efforts are desperate in their attempt to "both beg and boast" [1999, p. 10]. He [1999, p. 10] notes the dual message "in the same statement: 'Please pick us because we are wonderful.'" The very nature of such advertising suggests that prospective adoptive parents are seeking to comply with what Mansnerus [1998, p. A1] calls "the first commandment for couples wanting to adopt babies: Put yourselves across." Complying with that "commandment," however, tends to require brevity and panache, given the limited space allotted for making an impression in traditional advertising media. Consequently, many notices appear to make only the merest connection to the individuals' ability to parent. As Gritter [1999, p. 10] describes such advertising by prospective adoptive parents, they often are comprised of "whimsical three-sentence descriptions of an enterprising couple" in which image is elevated over substance and little more than the ardent desire to adopt is conveyed.

When a fuller presentation is possible—such as on the Internet or in presentations to birth parents arranged by lawyers or adoption agencies—prospective adoptive parents may have the opportunity to market themselves more thoroughly. Watson [1999, p. 7] observes that there is now "a host of ancillary exploiters, including public relations and marketing firms that help prospective adoptive parents prepare biographies and photographs to increase their appeal to birth parents." "And they do, in spunky performances on videotapes, in lush scrapbooks, and in professional portraiture smiling on the Internet" [Mansnerus 1998, p. A1]. One consultant, for example, advises prospective adoptive parents to attach "informal" pictures of themselves "enjoying one another" to their letters to birth parents; consider the use of "self-made or made-to-order tee shirts and pins as networking tools" to make their desire to adopt known to complete strangers; print business cards that include such messages as "We Want to Adopt a Baby!" and widely distribute them; and engage in almost relentless personal outreach to find the right connection that will lead to a baby [Lenington 1999]. Other consultants provide workshops at adoptive parents' conferences on topics such as writing "an empathic adoption ad" to "say what birthparents would like to hear" in a way that will cause the individual's ad to "stand out from others in the same newspaper" [Adoptive Parent Conference 1999]. Prospective adoptive parents are likely to be advised to highlight the financial and other material advantages which they, as adoptive parents, can bring to a child, thereby communicating to a birth mother that by selecting them, she will provide her child with a better life than she herself can offer [Pertman 1998].

Whether over the Internet or through personal advertising in newspapers or other publications, there is an "unaccountable realm of anonymity"[Gritter 1999, p. 10] that poses other issues. Contacts initiated and relationships forged through the medium of advertising take place without the filter of experienced professionals who may have the expertise and emotional distance to objectively assess the situation. Although some may argue that such direct contact has the benefit of removing intermediaries who overly control the adoption process and substitute their judgment for those of the parties themselves, others such as Gritter [1999, p. 10] fear that such contact provides unsettling opportunities for "emotional manipulation and financial extortion." Because of the power inequities inherent in infant adoption, discussed earlier, the potential dangers range from overreaching to exploitation.

The nature and scope of advertising by prospective adoptive parents raise important issues with ethical implications:

- Should individuals who wish to adopt have to "market" themselves in a public arena—to essentially "sell" themselves as a quality parenting product? Is marketing of one's qualifications to be a good adoptive parent essentially the same as or radically different than marketing one's professional or vocational skills?

- Should relationships leading to the adoptive placement of a child be instigated through the medium of advertising? Is advertising related to a desire to adopt the same as or different than personal advertising seeking a companion, a date, or a spouse?

- To what extent does advertising that highlights prospective adoptive parents' material advantages serve to further emphasize the financial inequities that generally characterize the group of people who adopt and the group of people who place their children for adoption?

- Finally, does such personal advertising have a tarnishing effect on the public perception of adoption? Does advertising, as Gritter [1999, p. 10] suggests, portray adoption not as a "well-reasoned, well-organized institution" but as "a mad scramble of desperate families clamoring for attention"?

Marketing and Children

"Marketing" children who need adoptive families is a concept that may stir a variety of reactions—from opposition based on a belief that such activity is too close to advertising to be acceptable to endorsement of these techniques as ways of ensuring a family for each child who needs adoption services and planning. Adoption practice has come to integrate a range of activities that feature children in a variety of venues and under a variety of circumstances. These activities have achieved variable levels of acceptance and, depending on the nature of the marketing under consideration, have raised questions with ethical implications.

Featuring Individual Children in Need of Adoptive Families

One aspect of marketing that features children takes the form of activities designed to inform the public about older children or children with physical, mental health or developmental problems who are in foster care and in need of adoptive parents. Children may be featured individually on local television programs—such as the *Wednesday's Child* programs currently being aired in Washington, D.C., New York City, and Chicago—or their photographs and limited descriptive information may be posted on Internet sites designed for this purpose—such as FACES of Adoption (www.adopt.org) or The Adoption Exchange (www.adoptex.org). Recognizing that these children are not the children avidly sought by large numbers of prospective adoptive parents who principally wish to adopt healthy infants, public child welfare agencies utilize these strategies in an attempt to personalize children in foster care in the hope of attracting adoptive parents who otherwise may not act upon an interest in adopting. In a less public venue, individual children also may be featured at "adoption parties" or "adoption fairs" attended by prospective adoptive parents who have already expressed an interest in adopting children in foster care and who are seeking a child for whom they would be the "right match" [Davis 2000].

These activities generally have enjoyed support, largely because they focus on the needs of children for whom traditional recruitment methods have not been successful and they involve no direct financial benefit to the parties involved. At the same time, the use of television programming and the Internet has been seen as an effective means of promoting the adoption opportunities of children who are "waiting." Local authorities in Great Britain, for example, recently posted a photograph of four young sisters on the Internet in an attempt to find a family who would adopt the sibling group [*The Guardian* 1999]. When newspaper publicity and other appeals failed to locate a family for the sisters, the agency made the decision to post their pictures on the Internet—a first in Great Britain. The agency representative stated, "We're just acknowledging that there is another more up-to-date medium for finding the families these children so desperately want—and the more opportunities you have, the best chance you have."

There are some, however, who express ethical concerns about the use of public media, including the Internet, for this purpose. Concerns are raised about the violation of the privacy of children featured in public forums and the "advertising" aura of such approaches. Schossler [1999], for example, raises questions related to the privacy interests of children when their pictures are displayed and information about the children's medical and social histories is posted. Do children who are featured on television or the Internet fully understand the potential impact of such publicity on their privacy? Salter [1999], for example, recounts how, as a child, he and his brother were featured on a television program in which adoptive parents were sought for them. He remembers, with embarrassment, his friends' jibes after seeing him on the television show and the pain that this loss of privacy caused. Cox [1999] contends that too little attention has been given to the issue of children's privacy—determining the extent to which identifying information (names and photographs) and nonidentifying information (social background and physical, mental health, and development needs) should be disclosed on the Internet and other public media. She urges that greater emphasis be placed on finding the appropriate balance between use of such media for recruitment purposes and protection of children's privacy interests.

Although clearly subject to some criticism on grounds of privacy, presentations of children in foster care waiting for adoptive families typically has generated less concern than the efforts of individuals to utilize the Internet to place their own or a client's child for adoption. Recent Internet activities of parents or facilitators attempting to place children for adoption in exchange for money illustrate the extent to which the medium is providing a new marketing environment. In one case, an adoptive mother attempted to place her eight-year-old Russian adopted daughter for adoption via the Internet. Using an adoption bulletin board to attract a prospective adoptive couple, she described her daughter as "very intelligent and very athletic" and asked for $4,000 in addition to transportation costs [Robinson & Kirksey 1999]. In another case, an adoption facilitator utilized an Internet service to attract prospective adoptive parents and subsequently demanded $60,000 for the baby, allegedly on behalf of a Hungarian woman who had brought her newborn to New York in hopes of finding an adoptive family for her [Hogan 1999b]. In a third case, a 14-year-old boy was allegedly sold over the Internet for $400 to a man who advertised his interest in adopting a "young boy who needs a dad" [Blum 1999].

As a variant of more traditional "child selling" or black market practices, these activities involving use of the Internet implicate the same ethical and legal issues associated with "trafficking" in children. They also raise the specter of broader opportunities for exploitation through marketing in an atmosphere of cyberspace anonymity. Addressing Internet advertising by both prospective adoptive parents and birth parents seeking to place their children, Schossler [1999] writes:

> What is more important is the element of "shopping" that the Internet encourages. The fact that a particular adoptive situation is presented with a price tag is the discomforting factor. The cost of adopting a child varies greatly ... Now, with the use of the Internet, these cost variations

are easily, and almost invariably, factored into an adoptive parent's decision to adopt a child. Children or birth mothers are compared by price. Adoptive parents are compared by their letters or pictures. This commodification of persons is not something that should be ignored by the adoption system.

Featuring Individual Children or Groups of Children by Demographic Characteristics

Children also may be "marketed" through use of advertising, as undertaken by some facilitators and adoption agencies, that specify the child's race and gender. An example of such activity is the Internet site maintained by a facilitator who posts children by race and gender, displaying this and other information on a grid that displays babies—identified by pseudonyms—whose birthdates fall within six months [www.adoptlink.com]. The first column of the grid specifies the race of the child and subsequent columns indicates gender, if known; the mother's prenatal health status; and fees for the adoption. When reviewed on January 17, 2000, the grid included a child, referred to as "Wes," who was described as "1/8 white, 1/8 Korean, 1/4 African American, and 1/2 Guianese" and whose gender was unknown. The adoption fee for this child was $10,900—$2,900 for the facilitator, $6,000 in living expenses for the mother, and $2,000 for the attorney. Another child, "Uca," a boy due in February 2000 was described as "1/2 white and 1/2 African American," and had an adoption fee estimated at $18,500, including the facilitator's fee. A third child, referred to as "Tab," also of unknown gender, was described as "white" and the fees for this child totaled $20,900—$2,900 for the facilitator, $15,500 for the "agency," and $2,500 for the "case worker."

Agency practice in this regard is not as stark. Watson [1999], however, points to some agencies' use of lists of the types of children which the agency places for adoption—lists which describe groups of children by race and/or gender and the fees charged for each such group. Typically, the highest fees are for Caucasian girls and the lowest fees for African American boys

[Watson 1999]. Though agencies often justify the lower fees for African American children as an effort to promote adoption by African American families whose incomes may be limited, there has been considerable criticism of both agencies' use of differential fees based on race and/or gender and the advertising of such fee structures [see Watson 1999].

The practice of specifying children's race and/or gender—either individually or as members of a group—gives rise to several questions with ethical implications:

- To what extent, if at all, is it appropriate to characterize children by race and/or gender for purposes of alerting prospective adoptive parents to their availability for adoption?

- Is there a justification for different fee levels for different groups of children? Does this practice reflect, in reality, an assessment of which children are more desirable and who can, therefore, generate a higher fee in a competitive environment?

- Does a differential fee structure suggest that non-Caucasian children, because they are "cheaper," are inherently less valuable? Does it suggest that if Caucasian adopters "settle" for a child of color, they should be compensated through a lower fee?

- To what extent, if at all, should lawyers', facilitators' or agencies' advertising incorporate such information as part of its marketing strategy? Does it present children in terms similar to the advertising of commodities of different brands or different makes and models—and sold at different prices?

The Child-Adoptive Parent "Match"

The extent to which a child may be viewed as "adoptable" may rest on how favorably the child is perceived by the agency itself and the prospective adoptive parents to whom he or she is presented. In contrast to an earlier era in which little health or other background information was collected or disclosed to adoptive parents, and the genetic and family history were deemed relatively insignificant, there currently is considerable emphasis on a child's genetic history and social background. As professionals and the general public have come to understand the impact of biological heritage as well as environmental conditions on a child's longer term health and development, prospective adoptive parents increasingly require considerable background information on any child that they might consider for adoption. Although the benefits of collection and disclosure of such information are readily recognized [Freundlich & Peterson 1998], issues arise as to the extent to which the current emphasis on collection and disclosure of health and other background information about a child suggests a growing preoccupation with locating perfect or near-perfect children who will satisfy the expectations of prospective adopters.

To the extent that such information is used to assist prospective adoptive parents in making a fully informed decision about adopting a particular child and to prepare adoptive parents to meet the child's future needs, it is likely to serve a positive, child- and family-centered purpose. To the extent, however, that the collection of health and other background information is designed to identify "perfect" children, at least in relation to the ideal as defined by prospective adopters, questions arise as to the ethics of a practice that may have strong marketing elements. Such questions include:

- Should an agency agree, at the request of prospective adoptive parents, to subject a child to genetic testing solely to assure them that the child does not present future health risks? Would it be acceptable to genetically test siblings and support an adoptive parent's decision to adopt the sibling with "good genes" and to reject the sibling with "bad genes"?

- Does the increasing attention to collection of health and other background information suggest that adoption is, to a growing extent, approximating the acquisition of a product that is accompanied by some guarantee or warranty?

- Alternatively, does the growing emphasis on collecting and disclosing genetic and other background information place birth parents in a position in which they must, to some degree, "market" themselves—as drug-free, as having no history of mental illness in the family, or as completely healthy?

Marketing by Adoption Service Providers

Individuals who offer adoption services are generally free to broadly advertise—in publications, in the yellow pages, on billboards, on buses, and through the Internet. Apart from the issue discussed earlier—facilitator and agency advertising that lists individual children or groups of children and their corresponding adoption fees—are questions related to the nature and scope of advertising designed to attract business—birth parents and prospective adoptive parents. This issue arises as an anomaly in the field of child welfare. With the exception of adoption, child welfare services generally have not been nor are they currently the subject of advertising. Child welfare services—such as child abuse and neglect investigations, foster care, and in-home counseling—are publicly-funded service, and agencies do not seek to generate an income stream based on privately-paid fees. By contrast, the adoption of infants in this country and the adoption of children from other countries by U.S. families are services for which agencies rely, to a significant extent, on fees paid by prospective adoptive parents (an issue discussed earlier). In order to continue to do business, agencies utilize advertising to attract prospective adoptive parents and, in domestic adoptions, birth parents. Similarly, business viability concerns shape the practice of advertising by lawyers and, where they may operate, by facilitators.

Assuming a legitimate business function associated with such advertising, the issue becomes one of the content of such marketing by both adoption agencies and attorneys. Are there themes typifying such marketing? And what do these advertising themes and methods suggest about adoption—from both the "business" and the professional perspective? In an attempt to better understand the content of marketing by adoption professionals, a review was conducted of the advertising sections of issues of *Adoptive Families* magazine published in 1998 and 1999 and of professional notices on the Internet. This review offers some indication of the nature of the advertising that may typify the contemporary marketing practices of adoption professionals.

Agency Advertising

The vast majority of advertisements in *Adoptive Families* were placed by agencies that exclusively offered international adoption services. Only a few agencies marketed themselves as specializing only in domestic infant adoption or as offering both "healthy U.S. newborns" and children from other countries. Agencies that principally provided international adoption services highlighted their geographic speciality—a single country or region of the world or multiple programs involving a variety of countries.

Some agencies—less than half—featured pictures of children in their advertisements, with considerable variation in the presentations. Some depicted happy smiling babies; others included close-up photos of older children; some advertisements offered descriptive titles under the pictures of children such as "Romanian princesses," "China dolls," and "Vietnamese beauties"; and others featured children swathed in lace, ribbons, and designer fabrics, or sporting cowboy hats or ethnic attire. One agency contrasted a child in her home country—in a picture in which she looks dirty and bedraggled—with her current situation, represented by a picture of her and her American adoptive mother in what appeared to be a "glamour shot." Some agencies avoided pictures altogether but promised quality children for quality families ["Our healthy babies need healthy families"].

Logos for adoption agencies were found to vary. One agency that specialized in adoptions of African children featured the continent of Africa over which was interposed a large eye from which a tear dropped. Another agency—which indicated that the agency specialized in "Caucasian newborns" but also offered programs placing "multicultural and biracial newborns"—depicted a stork in flight with a heart-shaped object dangling from its beak. Although some agencies used tag lines that focused on children ["Making a better life for children since 1972;" "Every child deserves a loving family;" "Thousands of orphans need loving families—can you help just one?"], others attempted to respond to adult frustrations and desires ("Are you still waiting?"; "Why are you still waiting?"; "Realize your dreams in nine months"; "This could be YOU!"). In a few cases, however, the agency's expectations of prospective adoptive parents were made clear ("Placement in Christian homes"). Others made adoption sound fun ("Experience the joy of adoption . . . internationally!"). Some suggested a fully stocked agency ("We now have children available from Russia)].

Few agencies committed themselves in their advertisements to short waiting times [notable exceptions were agencies promising placement in "2 to 6 months" and "3 to 9 months"] or provided cost information [an exception being the cost of an Ecuadorian adoption represented as "approximately $16,000"]. Some agencies, however, indicated the economy of their services through such representations as "inexpensive home studies."

The overall impression created by this advertising was mixed. Clearly, some agencies professionally presented information that conveyed a commitment to quality services for children and families. By contrast, however, the advertising of others—with the selected logos, pictures, and tag lines—conveyed a decidedly different message, ranging from pandering to paternalistic. In a disturbing number of cases, there was a marked consumer-oriented flavor in which children were glowingly presented as highly desirable products for "buying" customers. These agencies, apparently attempting to respond to the dynamics of the marketplace, utilized messages that appeared designed to tap into the thwarted desires and resources of prospective adoptive parents.

Attorney Advertising

Only a few independent practitioners—a limited number of lawyers and physicians—were found to advertise their services in *Adoptive Families*. Those attorneys who advertised in the publication highlighted their expertise and their personal status ["Proud adoptive parent"] and typically indicated that they offered a range of options that included not only adoption but surrogacy services as well. Attorneys were found to advertise more extensively on the Internet and, to some degree, in newspapers. One attorney promoted her services for prospective adoptive parents on the Internet with the assurance "*I really care*" [www.youcanadopt.info.htm (emphasis in original)]. In addition to extensive services for prospective adoptive parents (including "a search for a suitable birth parent") and for birth parents (who were assured "no charge and no obligation"), she—like attorneys advertising in *Adoptive Families*—offered surrogacy services. Other Internet sites contained testimonials from satisfied adoptive parents and birth mothers [see www.theshop.net/boren/birthmom.html]. In one newspaper notice [*USA Today* 1999, p. 10D], the lawyer provided birth parents who happened upon her advertisement with a glowing description of the benefits that prospective adoptive parents contacted through her office could provide to a child: "Storytelling/giggle sharing, cookie baker, t-ball, pony rides, YES!!"

It has also become apparent that attorneys from the United States have begun to advertise in newspapers in other countries, promoting their ability to provide European couples with "babies from the United States." A recent advertisement in a Swiss newspaper, for example, described a New York-based attorney's background in adoption law and invited Swiss couples to his "free lecture" at a Zurich hotel, promising applicants "short waiting periods" and emphasizing that "photos and medical records [are] available" [Keimer 1999]. In a similar vein, a North Carolina "adoption centre" promoted its services to Irish couples, offering to arrange the adoption of Russian children for $20,000 or more—a service about which Irish adoption groups have expressed significant criticism [O'Morain 1999].

The advertising by attorneys that was reviewed, like the marketing activities of agencies, varied in tone and message. Some advertising was quite professional. Other marketing was designed to convey the attorney's ability to quickly provide a quality product—with particular emphasis on speed and healthy newborns. Other advertising suggested an effort to convince prospective clients of the "softer side" of the legal profession. In these advertisements, emphasis was placed on the attorney's purported spirit of caring and personal commitment to adoption and included warm, if not sugar-coated, descriptions of the outcomes that the lawyers could readily achieve.

The advertising patterns observed among agencies and independent practitioners raise a number of issues. To what extent does marketing by adoption agencies and attorneys represent appropriate advertising? To what extent does such marketing play on the emotions of prospective adoptive parents or mislead prospective birth parents? Is it appropriate to use advertising techniques in adoption that may be effective in other product-oriented businesses—engaging photographs, catchy tag lines, bold logos, and promises of quick or economical results? Does this practice reflect commodification of children—or does it simply represent the realities of contemporary adoption practice?

Summary

Marketing has become endemic in adoption. Prospective adoptive parents—on their own and with the assistance of consultants, attorneys, and adoption agencies—market themselves as quality "parenting products." Children are marketed in a variety of ways: waiting children in foster care are featured on television or on the Internet in an effort to locate prospective adoptive parents; individual children are featured by parents or parent representatives on the Internet, often with a monetary figure associated with their offering for adoption; facilitators and agencies offer opportunities to adopt children of different races and genders at individual or group-assigned rates; and, increasingly, individual children are presented to individual prospective adoptive parents in product-based terms. Marketing by adoption professionals—agencies and lawyers—has expanded, both in form and venue. The content of advertising reflects a range of approaches, from professional presentations of child-focused services to promises of speedy results to meet the thwarted desires of adults. The Internet provides a range of new marketing opportunities and gives rise to new concerns, while the use of more traditional venues, such as newspapers and magazines for adoptive parents, also continues to grow.

As long as adoption has a business element, marketing will be a necessary component. It may play a positive role—in recruiting families for children when other efforts have failed, for example. It also, however, provides an unsettling picture of the realities of contemporary adoption practice and raises questions regarding the extent to which market forces will shape adoption in the future.

Conclusion

The debate is likely to continue regarding the role of market forces in shaping adoption policy and practice. Have these forces changed the inherent nature of adoption? Have children become commodified at some level, with the value of individual children dependent on age, intelligence, health, and developmental status, or intangible qualities such as physical attractiveness? Do adults have vested rights to "perfect" children, which adoption, as an enterprise, attempts to provide? The current environment raises a number of critical issues that must be addressed as adoption professionals consider practice and policy for the future. What will be the role of adoption in the future? Will its focus be on children who need families or on adults who wish to parent? Will adoption—in the end—be a "service," a "business," or some combination of aspirational and entrepreneurial intentions that perpetuate the tensions that characterize contemporary practice?

Serious challenges lie ahead if, as Watson [1999, p. 7] writes, "the sad truth is that we have lost our way in adoption. We are being driven by greed . . . We have all become victims of commercial exploitation—children, birth parents and siblings, adoptive parents, and those of us who tolerate this situation." Powerful market forces are in play, but, at the same time, professionals from all fields of adoption—infant adoption in the U.S., international adoption, and the adoption of children from the foster care system in this country—are raising questions about the ethics of current practice and challenging policies that may, in the past, have simply been tolerated. The environment indeed may be ripe for reshaping the forces that drive adoption.

References

Abma, J. C., Chandra, A., Mosher, W. D., Peterson, L. S., & Piccinino, L. J. (1997). Fertility, family planning and women's health: New data from the 1995 National Survey of Family Growth. *Vital Health Statistics, 23*(19), 1–35.

Adamec, C. (1999). News and Notes. *Adoption Medical News, 8,* 1–4.

Adoptive Parent Conference. (1999, November 14). How to write an empathetic adoption ad. Conference program for the 19th Annual Tri-State Adoption Conference. Mahwah, NJ.

Allen, M. (1999, May 31). Women accused of baby-selling used a friendly approach. *The New York Times,* pp. B1, B5.

Arizona Revised Statutes Annotated. (1999). Section 8-114 (A), (B).

Associated Press. (1998, January 30). Jury convicts woman of selling child now living in Chesapeake. *Virginia Pilot Ledger,* p. A12.

Associated Press. (1999, July 19). *U.N. studies international adoptions in Guatemala.* [Online]. Available: http:/cnn.com:80:/WORLD/americas/9...uatemala-UN-Adoption.ap/index.html [1999, July 29].

Avery, R. J. & Mont, D. M. (1994). *Special needs adoption in New York State: Final report on adoptive parent survey* (DHHS Contract No. 90CW1012). Washington, DC: U.S. Department of Health and Human Services.

Bachrach, C. A., London, K. A., & Maza, P. L. (1991). On the path to adoption: Adoption seeking in the United States, 1988. *Journal of Marriage and the Family, 53*(2), 705–718.

Barth, R. P. (1997). Effects of age and race on the odds of adoption versus remaining in long-term out-of-home care. *Child Welfare, 76*(2), 285–308.

Barth, R. P. & Berry, M. (1988). *Adoption and disruption: Rates, risks, and responses.* New York: Aldine de Gruyter.

Barth, R. P., Berry, M., Carson, M. L., Goodfield, R., & Feinberg, B. (1986). Contributors to disruption and dissolution of older-child adoptions. *Child Welfare, 65*(4), 359–371.

Bartholet, E. (1993). *Family bonds: Adoption and the politics of parenting.* New York: Houghton Mifflin Company.

Bartholet, E. (1996). International adoption: Propriety, prospects, and pragmatics. *Journal of American Academy of Matrimonial Lawyers*, 13(2), 181–210.

Baugher, E. & Lamison-White, L. (1995). *Poverty in the U.S.: 1995* (Current Population Reports, Series P60-194). Washington, DC: Bureau of the Census.

BBC News. (1999, March 28). *India adoption racket busted.* [Online}. Available: news.bbc.co.uk [1999, March 29].

Benet, M. K. (1976). *The politics of adoption.* New York: Free Press.

Berger, D. (1995). Improving the safety and efficiency of foreign adoptions: U.S. domestic adoption programs in other countries provide lessons for INS reform. *Journal of Law and Public Policy, 33*, 44.

Bernstein, N. (1999, December 4). City warns about shelter requirements. *New York Times*, p. B5.

Billingsley, A. (1993). *Climbing Jacob's ladder: The enduring legacy of African American families.* New York: Simon & Schuster.

Black Adoption Project. (1992). *Quarterly and Final Report, July 1– September 1, 1992.* (Grant #90C00468/01). On file with author.

Blum, J. (1999, October 17). Teen allegedly adopted through Internet. *Washington Post*, p. C4.

Boskey, J. B. & Hollinger, J. H. (1998). Placing children for adoption. In J.H. Hollinger (Ed.), *Adoption Law and Practice* (Vol. 1) (pp. 3-1 to 3-65). New York: Matthew Bender & Co.

Bouwma, R. (1999, September 27). Personal communication with Director, International Children's Services, Bethany Children's Services, Grand Rapids, Michigan.

Brown, E. G. & Bailey-Etta, D. (1997). An out-of-home care system in crisis: Implications for African American children in the child welfare system. *Child Welfare, 76*(1), 65–83.

Buffalo News. (1999, July 1999). Vietnam links 14 to adoption ring. *Buffalo News*, p. A2.

Calcetas-Santos, O. (1995). *Provisional report: Special rapporteur of the Commission on Human Rights on the sale of children, child prostitution, and child pornography.* U.N. Doc. A/50/456, 10.

Cantwell, N. (1983, March). The final document. International Children's Rights Monitor, 10–19.

Carro, J. L. (1995). Regulation of intercountry adoption: Can the abuses come to an end? *American Journal of Family Law, 9*, 135–153.

Carstens, C. & Julia, M. (1995). Legal, policy and practice issues for intercountry adoptions in the United States. *Adoption & Fostering, 19*(4), 26–33.

Chamberlain, P., Moreland, S. & Reid, K. (1992). Enhanced services and stipends for foster parents: Effects on retention rates and outcomes for children. *Child Welfare, 71*, 387–404.

Chandra, A., Abma, J., Maza, P., & Bachrach, C. (1999, May 11). Adoption, Adoption Seeking, and Relinquishment for Adoption in the United States. *Advance Data, 306.*

Child Protection Reports. (1999, November 11). Urban Institute affirms major changes still await nation's CW system. *Child Protection Report, 25*(23), 177–178.

Child Welfare League of America. (1994). *Kinship care: A natural bridge.* Washington, DC: CWLA Press.

Child Welfare League of America. (1995). *Child abuse and neglect: A look at the states.* Washington, DC: CWLA Press.

Child Welfare League of America. (2000). *Standards of excellence in adoption services.* Washington, DC: CWLA Press.

Child Welfare Watch. (1998). Child removals: Dislocating the black family. *Child Welfare Watch, 3*, 4–7.

Children's Clarion: Database on the rights of children. (1987). New York: Defense for Children International.

Children's Defense Fund. (1997). *The State of America's Children, Yearbook 1997.* Washington, DC: Children's Defense Fund.

Children's Defense Fund and National Coalition for the Homeless. (1998). Welfare to what: Early findings on family hardship and well-being. Washington, DC: Children's Defense Fund.

Cole Babies Website. (1999). [Online]. Available: http://www.afn.org/~w4gj/COLE.html [1999, September 2].

Courtney, M. E. (1997). The politics and realities of transracial adoption. *Child Welfare, 76*(6), 749– 780.

Courtney, M. E. (1999). Foster care and the costs of welfare reform. In P.A. Curtis, G. Dale, and J.C. Kendall (Eds.), *The foster care crisis* (pp. 129–151). Lincoln: University of Nebraska Press.

Cox, S. (1999, September 30). Personal communication. Director of Public Policy and External Affairs. Holt International Children's Services, Eugene, OR.

Crawford, J. M. (1999). Co-parent adoptions by same-sex couples: From loophole to law. *Families in Society: The Journal of Contemporary Human Services, 80*(3), 271–278.

Cummings, C. (1998). Adopting from Russia: A war of perceptions. *Russian Life, 41*(6), 1–9.

Dahl, B. (1999). Caring solutions: Holt-Vietnam Danang staff works with local officials to find effective ways to help children and families in crisis. *HI Families, 41*(4), 4–6.

Davis, D. (2000, January 17). Personal communication with the Executive Director, The Adoption Exchange, Aurora, CO.

DeFede, J. (1999, December/2000, January). How much for a white baby? *Talk,* 115–124.

Duryea, B. (1996, May 27). "Gray market" for adoptions emerges. *St. Petersburg Times,* p. 1B.

Edwards, D. (1999). American adoption and the experiences of relinquishing mothers. *Practicing Anthropology, 21*(1), 18–23.

English, D. & Clark, T. (1996). *Report of children in foster and group care placements in Washington State between June 1985 and August 1995.* Seattle, WA: Washington State Division of Children and Family Services, Office of Children's Administration Research.

Escobar, G. (1998, November 16). Lawyer's kidnap spotlights Louisiana adoption laws. *Washington Post,* p. C1.

The Evan B. Donaldson Adoption Institute (conducted by Princeton Survey Research Associates). (1997 November). *Benchmark Adoption Survey: Report on Findings.* New York: The Evan B. Donaldson Adoption Institute.

Evans, M. (1999, September 27). Personal communication with Executive Director, Joint Council of International Services for Children, Washington, D.C.

Flango, V. E. & Flango, C. R. (1995). How many children were adopted in 1992. *Child Welfare, 74*(5), 1018–1032.

Freundlich, M. (1997). The future of adoption for children in foster care: Demographics in a changing socio-political environment. *Journal of Children & Poverty, 3*(2), 33–61.

Freundlich, M. (1998). Supply and demand: The forces shaping the future of adoption. *Adoption Quarterly, 2*(1), 13–46.

Freundlich, M. (2000). *The role of race, culture, and national origin in adoption.* Washington, DC: CWLA Press.

Freundlich, M. & Peterson, L. (1998). *Wrongful adoption: Law, policy, and practice.* Washington, DC: CWLA Press.

Gilles, T. (1995). *Adoption assistance in America: A programmatic analysis fifteen years after federal implementation.* St. Paul, MN: North American Council on Adoptable Children.

Goerge, R. M., Wulczyn, F. H., & Harden, A. W. (1994). *Foster care dynamics, 1983–1992: California, Illinois, Michigan, New York and Texas. A report from the Multistate Foster Care Data Archive.* Chicago: University of Chicago, Chapin Hall Center for Children.

Goerge, R. M., Wulczyn, F. H., & Harden, A. W. (1995). *Foster care dynamics, 1983–1993: California, Illinois, Michigan, New York, and Texas—An update from the Multistate Foster Care Data Archive.* Chicago: Chapin Hall Center for Children, University of Chicago.

Gritter, J. (1999). The trend of commercialization in adoption. *Decree, 1,* 9–13.

Groze, V. (1985). Special needs adoption. *Children and Youth Services Review, 8,* 363–373.

Groze, V. (1991). Adoption and single parents: A review. *Child Welfare, 70*(3), 321–332.

Grunwald, M. (1997, February 26). State finds fewer want to fill foster parent role. *Boston Globe,* p. 2F.

The Guardian. (1999). Photos posted on the Net in adoption search. *The Guardian.* [Online]. Available: www.guardianunlimited.co.uk/Archive. [2000, January 12].

Halbfinger, D. M. (1999, May 28). U.S. accuses 3 of smuggling Mexican babies. *The New York Times,* pp. A1, B5.

Halfon, N., English, A., Allen, M. L., & De Woody, M. (1994). National health care reform, medicaid, and children in foster care. *Child Welfare, 73*(2), 99–115.

Harper, M. & Vandivere, S. (1999). *Poverty, welfare and children: A summary of the data. Child Trends Research Brief.* Washington, DC: Child Trends.

Hearings Before the Subcommittee on Children and Youth of the Committee on Labor and Public Welfare. (1975). 94th Congress, 1st Session.

Henley, J. (1999, May 5). *French check newborn adoption.* [Online]. Available: http:// detnews.com:80/1999/nation/9905/05/ 05050197.htm [1999, May 7].

Hermann, K. J. & Kasper, B. (1992). International adoption: The exploitation of women and children. *Affilia, 7*(1), 45–58.

Hester, M. (2000, February 6). Personal communication with Director of Adoption Services, The Barker Foundation, Cabin John, MD.

Hill, R. B. (1993). *Research on the African-American family.* Westport, CT: Auburn House.

Hogan, M. (1999a). Why the federal government must regulate adoption. *Decree, 1,* 1–5.

Hogan, S. (1999b, April 2). Stillwater couple helps New York police uncover adoption scam. *Star Tribune,* pp. A1, A14.

Hollinger, J. H. (1996). The Uniform Adoption Act: Reporter's ruminations. *Family Law Quarterly, 30*(2), 345–378.

Holtan, B. (1999, September 27). Personal communication, Director, Adoption Services, Tressler Lutheran Services, York, Pennsylavania.

Howard, M. (1984). Transracial adoption: Analysis of the best interests standard. *Notre Dame Law Review, 59,* 503–55.

Howe, R. A. W. (1995). Redefining the transracial adoption controversy. *Duke Journal of Gender, Law and Policy, 2,* 131–164.

Howe, R. A. W. (1997). Transracial adoption (TRA): Old prejudices and discrimination float under a new halo. *The Boston University Public Interest Law Journal, 6*(2), 409–472.

Howe, R.A.W. (2000, January 27). Personal correspondence. Professor Ruth-Arlene Howe, Boston College Law School, Newton Centre, MA.

Jacoby, N. (1999, April 5). *Financing an adoption.* [Online]. Available: cnnfn.com/1999/04/05/life/q_adoption/[2000, February 16].

Jacot, M. (1996). Adoption: For love or money? *The UNESCO Courier,* 2–4.

Jones, E. D. & McCurdy, K. (1992). The links between types of maltreatment and demographic characteristics of children. *Child Abuse and Neglect, 16*(2), 201–214.

Kalmuss, D. (1992). Adoption and black teenagers: The viability of a pregnancy resolution strategy. *Journal of Marriage and the Family, 54*, 485–495.

Kansas Legislative Services. (2000). House Bill No. 2747. [Online]. Available: http://www.ink.org/public/legislative/bills.cgi?billNum=2747&year=2000&doc=bill [2000, February 1].

Katz, J. (1999, May 5). In the adoption market, federal laws discriminate against the needy. *The Boston Globe*, p. A27.

Keimer, P. (1999, August 11). Correspondence to The Evan B. Donaldson Adoption Institute. On file at The Evan B. Donaldson Adoption Institute.

Kennard, H. C. (1994). Curtailing the sale and trafficking of children: A discussion of the Hague Convention in Respect to Intercountry Adoptions. *University of Pennsylvania Journal of International Economic Law, 14*(4), 623–650.

Kossoudji, S. A. (1989). Pride and prejudice: Culture's role in markets. In S. Shulman & W. Darity (Eds.), *The question of discrimination: Racial inequality in the U.S. labor market* (pp. 293–314). Middletown, CT: Wesleyan University Press.

Kroll, J. (1999a, Winter). 1998 U.S. adoptions from foster care projected to exceed 36,000. *Adoptalk*, 1–2.

Kroll, J. (1999b, Fall). Limited subsidies for adoptive families short-change children. *Adoptalk*, 1–2.

Kupenda, A. M. (1996–1997). Two parents are better than none: Single, African American adults—who are not in a traditional marriage or a romantic or sexual relationship with each other—should be allowed to jointly adopt and co-parent African American children. *Journal of Family Law, 35*, 703–720.

Landes, E. M. & Posner, R. A. (1978). The economics of the baby shortage. *Journal of Legal Studies, 7*, 323–48.

Lawrence-Webb, C. (1997). African American Children in the modern child welfare system: A legacy of the Flemming Rule. *Child Welfare, 76*(1), 9–30.

Lawyer accused in baby-selling racket. (1999, October 7). *The Province*, p. A2.

Lenington, S. (1999). *Networking.* [Online]. Available: www.adopting.org/network.html [1999, September 27].

Lind, M. (1998, August 16). The beige and the black. *New York Times Magazine*, pp. 38–39.

Lindsey, D. (1994). *The welfare of children.* New York: Oxford University Press.

Livingston, L. (n.d.). *International adoption: Report to and from the field.* Available from the National Adoption Information Clearinghouse, Washington, DC.

Lücker-Babel, M. F. (1990). *Intercountry adoption and trafficking in children: An initial assessment of the adequacy of the international protection of children and their rights.* Geneva, Switzerland: Defence for Children International.

McKenzie, J. (1993). Adoption of children with special needs. *The Future of Children, 3*(1), 62–76.

McRoy, R. G., Oglesby, Z., & Grape, H. (1997). Achieving same-race adoptive placements for African American children: Culturally sensitive practice approaches. *Child Welfare, 76*(1), 85–106

McTaggart, L. (1980). *The baby brokers.* New York: Dial Press.

Mandell, B. R. (1973). *What are the children? A class analysis of foster care and adoption.* Lexington, MA: Lexington Books.

Mansnerus, L. (1998, October 28). Market puts price tags on the priceless. *The New York Times*, pp. A1, A16–A17.

Marcenko, M.O. & Smith, L.K. (1991). Post-adoption needs of families adopting children with developmental disabilities. *Children & Youth Services Review, 13*(5–6), 413–424.

Martin, A. (1993). *The lesbian and gay parenting handbook.* New York: HarperCollins.

Maza, P. (1999, September 8). Personal communication with Director of Research, U.S. Children's Bureau, U.S. Department of Health and Human Services.

Meaker, P. P. (1989). Post-placement needs of adoptive families: A study of families who adopt through the Texas Department of Human Services. Master's Thesis, University of Texas at Arlington, Arlington, TX.

Meezan, W. (1980). Adoption services in the states. Washington, DC: U.S. Department of Health & Human Services.

Meezan, W., Katz, S., & Russo, E. M. (1978). *Adoptions without agencies: A study of independent adoptions.* New York: Child Welfare League of America.

Moffett, D. (1999, August 2). Sold when he was 8 days old, man seeks redress 47 years later. *Palm Beach Post,* p. 1A.

Mosher, W. D. & Bachrach, C. A. (1996). Understanding U.S. fertility: Continuity and change in the National Survey of Family Growth. *Family Planning Perspectives 28,* (1), 4–12.

Mosher, W. D. & Pratt, W. F. (1990). Fecundity and infertility in the United States, 1965–88. *Advance Data, 192,* 1–6.

Multi-Ethnic Placement Act of 1994. P. L. 103-382.

National Committee for Adoption. (1989). *Adoption factbook.* Washington, DC: National Committee for Adoption.

Neal, L. (1996). *The case against transracial adoption.* Focal Point, 10(1). [Online]. Available: www.rtc.pdx.edu/fp/spring96/transrac.htm [2000, February 16].

Nelson, K. (1985). *On the frontier of adoption: A study of special needs adoptive families.* New York: Child Welfare League of America.

Neubauer, R. (1988). Babies for sale. *World Press Review, 35*(8), 57.

North American Council on Adoptable Children. (1996). *User's guide to P.L. 96-272: A summarization and codification of administrative rulings.* St. Paul, MN: North American Council on Adoptable Children.

Oleck, J. (1999, July 9). *Mothers who think: All you need is love—and a marriage license.* [Online]. Available: http://www.salon.com/mwt/feature/1999/07/09/adoption/index.html [1999, July 12].

O'Morain, P. (1999, March 29). $20,000-plus scheme by U.S. adoption body is criticized. *Irish Times (Dublin),* p. 4.

Oppenheim, E., Bussiere, A., & Segal, E. C. (1999). Adoption assistance for children with special needs. In J. H. Hollinger (Ed.), *Adoption Law and Practice* (Vol. 2) (pp. 9-1 through 9-540). New York: Matthew Bender.

Ortiz, R. M. (1994). *Adopción Internacional o tráfico de niños: Paraguay.* Asunción, Paraguay: Centro de Documentacion y Estudios.

Pahz, J. A. (1988). The ethicality of child-finding in third world countries for the purpose of adoption. *International Quarterly of Community Health Education, 8*, 219–222.

Pastor, R. (1989, May). The Honduran baby market. *Sojourner: The Women's Forum, 19*, 15.

Parks, C. A. (1998). Lesbian parenthood: A review of the literature. *American Journal of Orthopsychiatry, 68*(3), 376–389.

Pearlman-Smith, E. (1989). *The relationship of services to success in older child adoption.* Ph.D. Thesis, Yeshiva University, New York.

Pelton, L. & Milner, J. (1994). Is poverty a key contributor to child maltreatment? In E. Gambrill & T. J. Stein (Eds.), *Controversial Issues in Child Welfare* (pp. 16–28). Needham Heights, MA: Allyn & Bacon.

Pertman, A. (1998, March 9). Vying to be among the chosen. Boston Globe, pp. A1, A10–A11.

Perry, T. L. (1998). Transracial and international adoption: Mothers, hierarchy, race and feminist legal theory. *Yale Journal of Law and Feminism, 10*, 101–164.

Petit, M. R. & Curtis, P. A. (1997). *Child abuse and neglect: A look at the states (1997 CWLA Stat Book).* Washington, DC: CWLA Press.

Pilotti, F. J. (1993). Intercountry adoption—Trends, issues and policy implications for the 1990s. In *Childhood* (Vol. I)(pp. 165–177). Montevideo, Uruguay: Instituto Interamericano del Niño.

Posner, R. A. (1992). *Sex and reason.* Cambridge, MA: Harvard University Press.

Ramsey, C. (1999, May 19). Do you need adoption insurance? *Kansas City Star*, p. F6.

Riccardi, N. (1999, July 31). Woman allegedly offers baby for adoption 7 times. *The Los Angeles Times*, p. 1.

Ricketts, W. & Achtenberg, R. (1990). Adoption and foster parenting for lesbians and gay men: Creating new traditions in family. *Journal of Homosexuality, 3*, 83–116.

Rios-Kohn, R. (1998). Intercountry adoption: An international perspective on the practice and standards. *Adoption Quarterly, 1*(4), 3–32.

Rivera, R. (1999, October 29). Lawsuit challenges policy that restricts adoptions. *The Salt Lake Tribune.* [On-line]. Available: http://www.sltrib.com:80/1999/oct/10291999/utah/42403.htm [1999, December 23].

Robinson, K. (1996, June 23). Q/A: Answers to questions about foreign adoptions. *The Idaho Statesman*, p. 5D.

Robinson, M. & Kirksey, J. (1999). Mother accused of selling daughter online. Denver Post. Available on-line: http://www.denverpost.com:80/news/news05251.htm [1999, May 25].

Romanchik, B. (1996, Summer). The benefits of open adoption. *Open Adoption: Birthparent, 9*, 1–7.

Rosenthal, J., Schmidt, D. & Conner, J. (1988). Predictors of special needs adoption disruption: An exploratory study. *Children and Youth Services Review, 10*, 101–117.

Rothschild, M. (1988, January). Babies for sale. *The Progressive*, 18.

Ruane, M. E. & Shaver, K. (1998, November 12). Puzzling case of adoption specialist; lawyer in alleged abduction also called a hero, a pioneer. *Washington Post*, p. A1.

Salter, S. (1999, October 4). Keynote Address, Best Child Welfare Practices Symposium, Maryland Department of Human Resources, Baltimore, MD, October 4–5, 1999.

Sandor, G. (1994, June). The "other" Americans. *American Demographics*, 36–42.

Schemo, D. J. (2000, February 12). Despite options on census, many to check "Black" only. *New York Times*, pp. A1, A10.

Schossler, T. (1999). Abstract. *Virtual babies: The adoption market and the role of the Internet.* Presentation at Ethics and Adoption: The Challenges for Today and the Future, conference presented by The Evan B. Donaldson Adoption Institute. Anaheim, CA. November 3–5, 1999.

Sedlak, A. & Broadhurst, D. (1992). *Study of adoption assistance impact and outcomes: Final report.* (Contract No. 105-89-1607, Westat, Inc). Washington, DC: U.S. Department of Health and Human Services.

Serrill, U. S. (1991, October 21). Going abroad to find a baby. *Time*, 86.

Shapiro, E. D. & Schultz, L. (1985/1986). Single-sex families; The impact of birth innovations upon traditional family notions. *Journal of Family Law, 24*, 271–281.

Shireman, J.F. (1995). Adoptions by single parents. In S.M.H. Hanson et al. (Eds.) *Single Parent Families: Diversity, myths and realities* (pp. 367–388). Binghamton, NY: The Haworth Press, Inc.

Sokoloff, B. Z. (1993). Antecedents of American adoption. *The Future of Children: Adoption 3*(1), 17–25.

Sollinger, R. (1992). *Wake up little Susie: Single pregnancy and race before* Roe v. Wade. New York: Routledge.

Sorosky, A. D., Baran, A., & Pannor, R. (1979). *The adoption triangle: The effects of the sealed record on adoptees, birth parents, and adoptive parents.* Garden City, NY: Anchor Books.

Stanfield, N. (2000). The commercialization of Emily (describing House Bill 2747 introduced in the Kansas State Legislature by Rep. Thomas Klein). [Online]. Available: adoption.about.com/parenting/adoption/library/weekly/aa013100b.htm?terms+House+Bill+2747.

Stolley, K. S. (1993). 1993 Statistics on adoption in the United States. *The Future of Children: Adoption, 3*(1), 26–42.

Sullivan, A. (1999, December 1). Personal communication with Director of Adoption Services, Child Welfare League of America, Washington, D.C.

Sullivan, A. (2000, January 17). Personal communication with Director of Adoption Services, Child Welfare League of America, Washington, D.C.

Super, D. A., Parrott, S., Steinmetz, S., & Mann, C. (1996, 13 August). *The new welfare law.* Washington, DC: Center on Budget and Policy Priorities.

Tasker, F. L. & Golombok, S. (1997). *Growing up in a lesbian family.* New York: Guilford Press.

Tatara, T. (1993). Voluntary Cooperative Information System (VCIS): Characteristics of children in substitute and adoptive care (based on FY 82 through FY 90 data). Washington, DC: American Public Welfare Association.

Tennessee Black Market Adoption Information. (1999, September 2). Available: http://www.geocities.com/Heartland/Bluffs/3592/TNBMA.html [1999, December 23].

Terpstra, J. (2000, January 17). Personal communication with former Child Welfare Services Specialist, U.S. Children's Bureau, Washington, D.C.

Testa, M. F., Shook, K. L., Cohen, L. S., & Woods, M. G. (1996). Permanency planning options for children in formal kinship care. *Child Welfare, 75*(5), 451–470.

Triseliotis, J. (1993). Inter-country adoption: In whose best interests? In M. Humphrey & H. Humphrey (Eds.), *Inter-country adoption: Practical experiences* (pp. 119–137). London: Routledge.

Tyree, W. (1999, June 9). The business of international adoption. *The Japan Times*, pp. 1–5.

UNICEF International Child Development Centre. (1998). *Intercountry adoption*. Florence, Italy: Author.

United States Bureau of Census. (1994). *Fertility of American women: June 1994*. Washington, DC: U.S. Government Printing Office.

U.S. Bureau of the Census. (1998). Current Population Reports, Series P-25, No. 311, Estimates of the Population of the United States by Single Years of Age, Color, and Sex: 1900 to 1959; Series P-25, No. 519, Estimates of the Population of the United States by Single Years of Age, Sex and Race: April 1, 1960 to July 1, 1973; SeriesP-25, No. 917, Preliminary Estimates of the Population of the United States by Single Years of Age, Sex and Race: 1970 to 1981; Series P-25, No. 1130, Population Projections of the united States by Age, Sex, Race, and Hispanic Origin: 1995 to 2050.

U.S. Department of Health and Human Services. (1992). *The National Survey of Current and Former Foster Parents*. Prepared under contract number: 105-89-1602. Washington, DC: U.S. Department of Health and Human Services, Children's Bureau.

U.S. Department of Health and Human Services. (1996, August 7). *Summary of provisions: Personal Responsibility and Work Opportunity Reconciliation Act of 1996 (H.R. 3734)*. Washington, DC: U.S. Department of Health and Human Services, Office for the Assistant Secretary for Planning and Evaluation.

U.S. Department of Health and Human Services. (1999). *The AFCARS Report: Current Estimates as of March 1999*. Washington, DC: U.S. Department of Health and Human Services, Administration for Children and Families. [Online]. Available: www.acf.dhhs.gov/programs/cb [1999, December 28].

U.S. Department of Health and Human Services. (2000). *The AFCARS Report: Current Estimates as of January 2000*. Washington, DC: U.S. Department of Health and Human Services, Administration for Children and Families. [Online]. Available: http://www.acf.dhhs.gov/programs/cb/stats/tarreport/rpt0100/ar0100.htm [2000, March 2].

U.S. General Accounting Office. (1994). *Foster care: Parental drug abuse has alarming impact on young children.* Washington, DC: U.S. General Accounting Office.

U.S. House of Representatives. (1996). *1996 Green Book.* Washington, DC: U.S. House of Representatives, Committee on Ways and Means.

United States Information Agency. (1994). *The "baby parts" myth: The anatomy of a rumor.* Washington, DC: United States Information Agency.

USA Today. (1999, September 16). Classified Advertisements, p. 10D.

Vermont Statutes Annotated. (1999). Title 15A, Section 7-103.

Vobejda, B. (1996, November 27). Family characteristics appear more stable. *The Washington Post,* p. A03.

Voice for Adoption. (1997, February). *Washington Update,* 5.

Walliser, T.L. (1997). *My two dads: New Jersey legalizes gay adoption; ACLU's battle moves on.* ABC News.com.

Watson, K. W. (1992, Winter). Providing services after adoption. *Public Welfare,* 5–12.

Watson, K. W. (1999). Who cares if people are exploited by adoption? *Decree, 1999* (1), 7–8.

Wegar, K. (1997). *Adoption, identity, and kinship.* New Haven: Yale University Press.

Weidermeier-Bower, J. (1997). *The adoption subsidy maximum basic rates: 1996 survey.* St. Paul, MN: North American Council on Adoptable Children.

Woman searching for past finds black market in babies doctor engineered illegal adoption of 200 infants. (1997, July 20). *St. Louis Post Dispatch,* p. B4.

www.adopting.org. (1999, September 6). Newsletter for Week of September 6.

Zelizer, V. A. (1985). *Pricing the priceless child: The changing social value of children.* Princeton: Princeton University Press.

About the Author

Madelyn Freundlich is the executive director of The Evan B. Donaldson Adoption Institute. She is a social worker and lawyer whose work has focused on child welfare policy and practice for the past decade. She formerly served as general counsel for the Child Welfare League of America and as associate director of Program and Planning for the Massachusetts Society for the Prevention of Cruelty to Children. She is the author of a number of books and articles on child welfare law, policy, and financing. Her most recent writing has focused on the impact of welfare reform on foster care and special-needs adoption, interstate adoption law and practice, genetic testing in adoption evaluations, and confidentiality in adoption law and practice. Ms. Freundlich received her master's degrees in social work and public health, and she also holds a J.D. and LL.M.

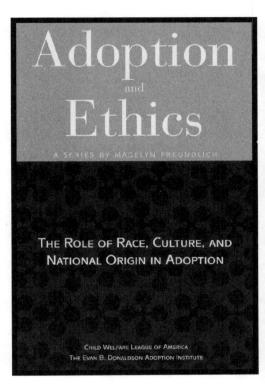

The Solent

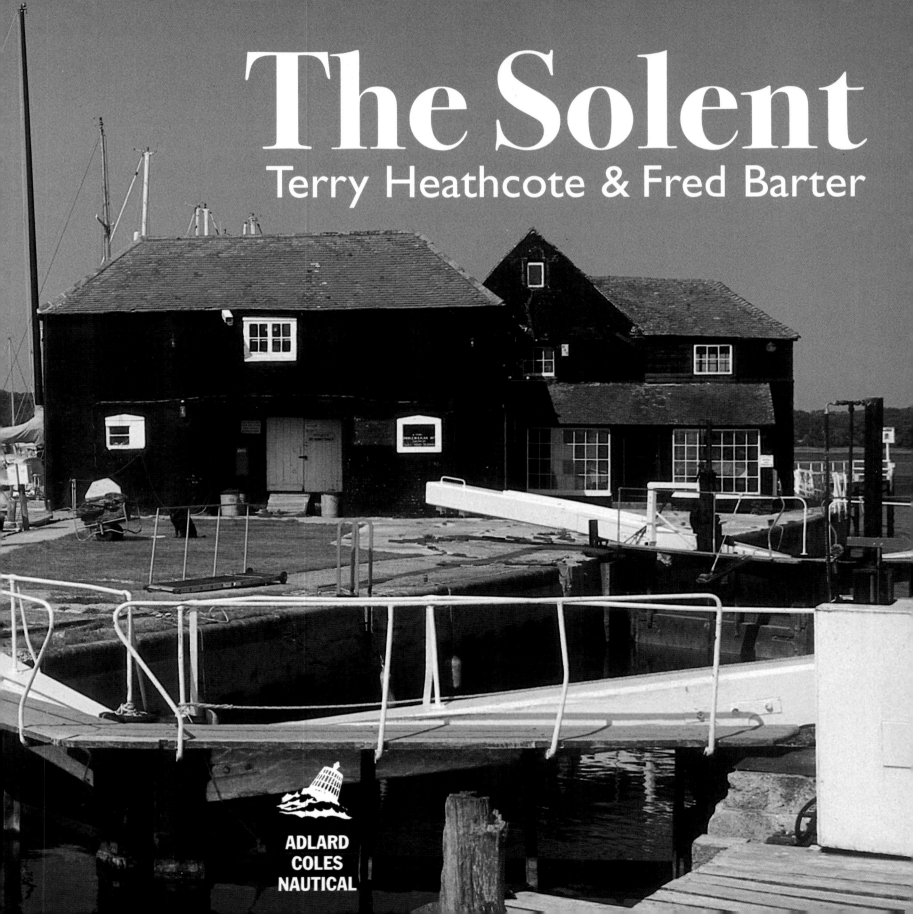

The Solent
Terry Heathcote & Fred Barter

ADLARD
COLES
NAUTICAL

Contents

This book is divided into the five sections shown below.
The Introduction is on page 6.
The Index is on page 159.

Published by Adlard Coles Nautical
an imprint of A & C Black Publishers Ltd
38 Soho Square, London W1D 3HB
www.adlardcoles.com

Copyright
© Photography – Terry Heathcote
© Introduction – Keith Hill
© Text – Fred Barter

First edition 2008

ISBN 978-1-4081-0378-4

This book is produced using paper that is made
from wood grown in managed, sustainable forests.
It is natural, renewable and recyclable. The logging and
manufacturing processes conform to the environmental
regulations of the country of origin.

Typeset in 9pt Gill Sans light
Printed and bound in
Singapore by Star Standard Industries (Pte) Ltd

Designed by Fred Barter,
The Bosun Press.

1. New Forest Coast

2. Southampton Water

3. Portsmouth Harbour

4. Chichester Harbour

5. Isle of Wight

Introduction

Readily recognisable from the diamond-shaped Isle of Wight, the Solent shore is situated in central southern England. Around 75% of the mainland, or northern, shore lies within Hampshire, only the eastern extremity belonging to West Sussex. The whole of the southern shore is formed of the Isle of Wight's northern coastline.

A chalk ridge once linked the Isle of Wight to the Old Harry Rocks near Studland but it was eventually breached. This took place around 3,000 years ago and created the now familiar outline of the Solent and the Isle of Wight. The Needles stand today as a reminder of this former landscape.

The predominantly eastward drift of the sea through the Solent has given rise to great shingle banks, such as those at Hurst and Calshot. The shallow, sheltered waters thus created led to development of extensive mudflats and salt marsh, the preferred habitat of so many of the Solent's wild creatures.

So far as wildlife is concerned, some changes have been fairly rapid. Obviously there has been the loss of certain species, largely due to human interference, but there have also been gains. An excellent example is the Little Egret, a pure white bird with elegant plumes and comical yellow feet. The guidebooks of 15 years ago described its range as extending northward to central France. Not any longer. A population explosion saw the Little Egret push across the Channel to establish itself along favoured stretches of the Solent shore.

The wildfowl and wading birds of the Solent shore have a pivotal role to play in making it such a special place. The glittering prize for turning out on a cold but sunny winter day is to see them wheeling around in their thousands, dazzling in their aerial supremacy and glowing with vibrant colour. Favoured spots are Chichester Harbour, Farlington Marshes and Keyhaven, or the harbours at Newtown or Bembridge.

In the summer months it is the flowering plants that steal the show. Shingle shores offer the brilliance of the Yellow Horned Poppy, along with the Sea Kale, whose young white stalks were a delicacy for centuries.

With its great diversity of habitats and wildlife, the Solent shore merits appropriate protection. And it gets it. Nearly 80% of the coastline enjoys some form of protected status. With effect from March 2005, part of the Solent shore entered a new dimension when it was brought within the New Forest National Park.

There has always been a rich seam of history to be mined along the Solent shore. The busy port of Southampton, and Chichester, which sleeps contentedly under the shadow of its fine cathedral, can both trace their origins back to Roman times. Meanwhile, the sheer walls of the fort at Portchester Castle survey Portsmouth Harbour, while reflecting on their status as being amongst the finest remaining examples of Roman fortifications in northern Europe. At the head of the easternmost channel of Chichester Harbour, meanwhile, lies the Roman palace at Fishbourne.

The Bayeux Tapestry depicts King Harold arriving at Bosham's Saxon church, but hard evidence of the Norman conquest along the Solent shore is limited. There is little more than the remains of the castle at Southampton and the Norman tower built within the Roman castle at Portchester. More recent territorial disputes, particularly with France, led to the Solent being sprinkled with a range of fortifications and castles: some are handsome structures; others less so.

Southampton's splendid Bargate and well preserved city walls speak of brutish times. In 1415 the young Henry V passed this way with his illustrious bowmen on the way to victory against the odds at Agincourt. At the end of the 15th century, Portsmouth was established as Britain's premier naval base. It came to prominence following rejection of the Catholic Church by Henry VIII and dissolution of the monasteries, seminal events with an inevitable consequence – the threat of invasion by France and Spain.

A rash of fortifications quickly followed, partly funded by the dissolution of three Solent shore monasteries: Netley on Southampton Water, Beaulieu at the head of its eponymous river and Quarr near the entrance to Wootton Creek. The castles at Calshot, Cowes, Hurst, Southsea and Yarmouth all bear witness to this period of history.

The Solent shore has very famous associations with Admiral Lord Nelson, hero of Trafalgar. Portsmouth proudly hosts his superbly restored flagship *Victory*.

With the arrival of European unity, the threat of invasion dissipated. The focus of the Solent shore switched instead to conservation of its natural resources and, of course, leisure. Any fine day sees an array of brightly coloured yacht sails and the white V-wakes of powered craft. Sheltered waters, unusual double tides and a profusion of navigable channels and creeks make the Solent one of the most popular boating centres in the country.

Bringing order to the apparently random movements of leisure craft are great container ships and cruise liners serving Southampton, a city that has always drawn its lifeblood from the sea, along with naval vessels and Continental ferries plying to and from Portsmouth. Busy ferries provide an essential lifeline between the Isle of Wight and the mainland. Fast passenger services link Ryde with Portsmouth and West Cowes with Southampton. Vehicle ferries, meanwhile, shuttle between Fishbourne and Portsmouth, East Cowes and Southampton, and from Yarmouth to Lymington.

Public transport generally has kept the Solent shore in the headlines over the years, sometimes for the wrong reasons. For example, the 'unsinkable' *Titanic* left Southampton in 1912 on a maiden voyage that was to end in well-documented tragedy.

Hythe was also the test bed for Sir Christopher Cockerell's hovercraft concept, examples of which still provide a regular service between Southsea and Ryde.

Meanwhile, railway services provided to and from the Solent shore continue to mesh seamlessly with the ferries. They range from the Island Line museum piece, along which 1938-built ex-London Underground trains run between Ryde Pier Head and Shanklin, via the 'heritage' trains of the Community Railway to and from Lymington, to the state-of-the-art 'Desiro' electric trains that began revolutionising Portsmouth and Southampton services with effect from 2005.

The Solent shore may have had a fascinating and sometimes troubled past; but it also has a bright future. Portsmouth's magnificent Spinnaker Tower stands as a sparkling icon of a new era, and it reflects the region's commitment to building on past achievements in order to scale new heights.

Keith Hill

1. The New Forest Coast

The New Forest Coast includes freshwater lagoons, salt marsh, shingle, tidal mudflats, wooded coastal lowlands and the estuaries of the Beaulieu and Lymington rivers. Those wishing to experience the New Forest Coast in person can follow the route from Keyhaven and visit the marshes and former saltings and then on to the port and sailing centre of Lymington.

From Lymington you can head inland through the New Forest and the villages of Bucklers Hard and Beaulieu to Hythe on the west bank of Southampton Water. From Hythe you can take the ferry across Southampton Water to the Town Quay in the centre of the port city.

Keyhaven

Right
Fishing boats - Keyhaven in January

Keyhaven is the most westerly port in the Solent, protected by the hook-shaped Hurst beach with Hurst Castle guarding the western entrance to the Solent. It is possible that the name Keyhaven came from the Saxon 'cy-haefenn' which means 'the harbour where the cows are shipped'.

These fishing boats nestle quietly together ready for their next trip to sea.

The mainly eastward drift of the sea through the Solent has given rise to great shingle banks, such as those at Hurst and Calshot. The shallow, sheltered waters led to the development of extensive mudflats and salt marsh, the preferred habitat of so many of the Solent's wild creatures.

The shingle spur of Hurst Spit reaches out towards the Isle of Wight. At its tip is Hurst Castle, grim and remote, a reminder of a troubled past. King Charles I was imprisoned in the old round castle before being taken to the scaffold. A handful of cottages were once occupied by a community who shared this outpost as their home.

Between Hurst Castle and Keyhaven a regular summer ferry threads its way between the mudflats. In winter it becomes the exclusive domain of wildfowl and wading birds. The seawall walk to Lymington offers views across shimmering salt marsh to the restless Solent, and placid lagoons inland – a birdwatcher's paradise.

Previous pages
Beaulieu River - Dawn in December

Left

The Quay, Lymington

Any fine day sees an array of brightly coloured yacht sails on the water and the white V-wakes of motor boats. Sheltered waters, plus the unusual double tides and a profusion of navigable channels and creeks make the Solent one of the most popular boating areas in the country.

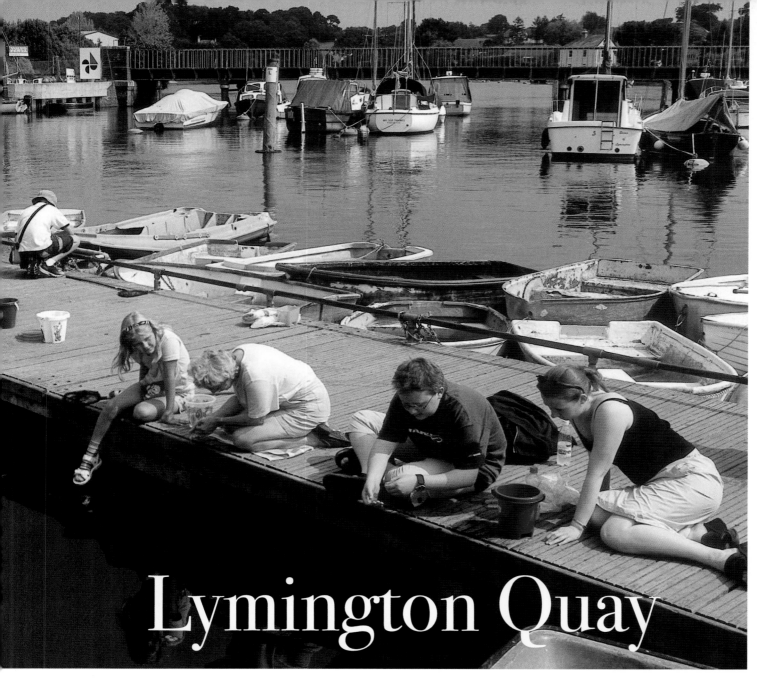

Lymington Quay

Above

Crabbing at the Quay

Lymington has always been associated with ships and the sea. It was from here in 1790 that HMS *Pandora* sailed to the Pacific in search of the mutineers from the *Bounty*. In earlier times Lymington made its living from boatbuilding, iron smelting, oyster dredging and salt processing. Nowadays the profusion of yacht masts tell a different story.

At one time piracy flourished here, eventually being superceded by the less dangerous practice of smuggling.

Lymington Town Quay is close by the lower part of the town and there are a plethora of mooring buoys and pontoon berths. There are often so many boats that they sometimes have to tie up alongside each other, known in yachting terms as 'rafting up'.

Above

Captain's Row, Lymington

Captain's Row once had the reputation of being too dangerous to walk. If the weather was bad, the local fishermen were inclined to behave badly, maybe because of much time being spent in the King's Head on Quay Hill. This pub has over 300 years of history and it once shared space on the street with opium dens and brothels.

Lymington Town

Above

Quay Street, Lymington

The Georgian facades of the buildings in Lymington are distinctive. It was founded as a new town in about 1200, and today they provide a beautiful backdrop for the pleasures of shopping. Quay Street is a mixture of gift and fashion shops and restaurants. It has changed little over the centuries; the cobbles help prevent sliding down the steep descent to the waterside.

Lymington River

Above

The Quay, Lymington

The river today has little commercial traffic, apart from the Wightlink ferries crossing to Yarmouth. These are very big in comparison to the yachts and other small boats seen here. At one time earlier ferries were flat-bottomed and known as 'hoys', maybe leading to the expression 'ship ahoy'.

Above

Coastal marsh, near Oxey

Lymington has also known the smoke and grime of industry, its speciality being salt production. Seawater flooded a series of salt pans and was allowed to evaporate, the resultant brine being boiled in coal-fired furnaces. By the mid 18th century some 6,000 tons were being produced annually.

The industry's collapse was heralded by the prohibitive cost of bringing in coal, coupled with larger scale production in Cheshire.

Oxey Marsh

Left

Oxey coastal marsh in November

Oxey and Pennington marshes are where at one time the local salt industry produced 6,000 tons a year. Old salt pans are still visible from the sea wall, but where there was brine there are now birds, including Goldeneye, Eiders, Red-breasted Mergansers and Great Crested Grebes.

Right
Beaulieu Estate in January

The name 'Beaulieu' means beautiful place. The estate has been owned by the Montagu family for four centuries. The tranquility they have established can be clearly seen in this photograph.

The great abbey, founded here during the reign of King John, was dissolved by Henry VIII. The former 14th century Great Gatehouse of Beaulieu Abbey, Palace House, is set in glorious grounds and gardens overlooking the Beaulieu River. The House has belonged to Lord Montagu's family since 1538, when Sir Thomas Wriothesley, later 1st Earl of Southampton, bought the Estate after the Dissolution of the Monasteries. The architect was Sir Arthur Blomfield and the House is a mixture of Victorian Gothic, medieval Gothic and 18th century fortification styles.

The meandering Beaulieu River takes us past Bucklers Hard. Here, an incredibly wide street of delightful red brick cottages is inclined towards the water, where great ships for Nelson's navy were built of New Forest oak. Beaulieu village sits at the head of the river's tidal reach.

The Beaulieu Estate

Above
The mill pond in January

The river rises near Lyndhurst and flows south easterly across the forest heaths to the village of Beaulieu. It is 12 miles long, of which the last 4 miles are tidal. The entire river, including its bed, is owned by Lord Montagu of Beaulieu.

The river at one time drove a tide mill in the village, and it continues to flow through the forest, entering the sea through the Solent.

Right
The Beaulieu River in February

Beaulieu River

Exbury Gardens

Above
Beaulieu Abbey ruins in April

The great glory of the Beaulieu River's east bank is Exbury
Gardens, a blaze of colour when its azaleas and rhododendrons
are in bloom. The garden was created by Lionel Nathan de
Rothschild. He described himself as a gardener by profession
with banking as a hobby. He bought the Exbury Estate in
1919, which the previous owner had described as an 'earthly
paradise'. With its temperate climate and moderate rainfall,
the acidic soil is ideal for growing rhododendrons.

Left
Exbury Gardens in May

Inchmery

Top right
Bait digging in May

Inchmery is very close to Exbury and Lepe Country Park. At low tide this shore is exposed to extensive mudflats. The park affords wonderful views of the Solent and the Isle of Wight. The mud provides feeding grounds for many bird species including Curlew, Oystercatcher, Dunlin and Plover.

Above
Turnstone, Lepe beach in January

Left
Coast erosion/protection, Inchmery in September

Above
Coastguard cottages, Lepe in September

In the 1870s an embryonic scheme was drawn up for a railway tunnel from Stone Point, burrowing beneath the Solent to Cowes. That idea may have been stillborn, but the area thrives today as Lepe Country Park. The Park occupies a narrow stretch of land adjoining the Solent, just west of Southampton Water and south of the New Forest, and lies within an Area of Outstanding Natural Beauty. With habitat ranging from mudflats to shingle, it is a haven for coastal flowering plants and shorebirds. There are also reminders of World War II. Sections of the floating 'Mulberry' harbours were made here, prior to playing their part in the D-Day landings. A suitable memorial records Lepe's wartime significance. Lepe is also a popular venue for watching the firework spectacular that marks the end of Cowes Week in August each year.

Right
Towards Cowes from Lepe County Park in September

Lepe Country Park

Southampton Water

Top right
The Old Power Station from Calshot marshes in December

At the entrance to Southampton Water is Calshot shingle spit. It is busy with beach huts, huge hangars, a lifeboat station, and an old RAF base now used as an activities centre. A Tudor fort is juxtaposed with a radar tower. A muddle it may be, but it provides the ideal spot from which to observe deep sea shipping. Southampton Water is classified geographically as a ria, or drowned valley. Formed by the rivers Test, Itchen and Hamble, it became an inlet of the sea at the end of the last ice age, at which point sea levels rose causing flooding to many valleys in the South of England. The resulting depth of water in Southampton plus the soft silt of the river-bed, which allows for comparatively easy dredging, has provided an ideal venue for visiting ships over the years. The additional phenomenon of the 'double tide' enables prolonged periods of high water, thus greatly facilitating the movement of large ships.

Above
Calshot Activities Centre from Calshot marshes in December

Left
Commercial shipping and the Isle of Wight ferry to Lepe in January

Above

Calshot Castle and radar tower in September

Calshot Castle is one of Henry VIII's device forts, built on Calshot Spit at the Solent near Fawley to guard the entrance to Southampton Water. Device Forts were artillery fortifications built by the King. Fear of invasion from France and Spain came when Henry divorced Catherine of Aragon in 1538.

The castle was built as a circular blockhouse with a three storey central keep in 1540 using stone from Beaulieu Abbey. The outer walls were lowered in 1774 and the gatehouse was rebuilt in order to provide more living space. The south east battery was added in 1895 but has since been demolished. The castle was in use until 1956.

Right

Sea kale at Calshot Spit in June

The one-mile long Calshot Spit is located on the southern bank of the open end of Southampton Water.

The Calshot Naval Air Station was located here because it is sheltered by land on three mainland sides plus the Isle of Wight as a fourth.

The spit is a potential hazard to navigation, and vessels entering Southampton Water are warned of it by the Calshot Spit light float, a distinctive navigational mark..

Calshot

2. Southampton Water

From Southampton you can cross the River Itchen by the high-level Itchen Bridge and follow the northern shore of Southampton Water past Netley Castle to the ruins of Netley Abbey, and the Royal Victoria Country Park. If you go on further you will reach the yachting centre of Hamble-le-Rice. Here you can cross the River Hamble on the small pedestrian Hamble-Warsash Ferry to the village of Warsash.

Hythe

Above

Hythe Marina in May

Leaving behind Calshot Castle, guardian of Southampton Water, you enter a world of industry and high density housing. And yet there are unexpected gems that have survived relatively unscathed. Ashlett Creek is tucked improbably between a power station and the great refinery complex at Fawley. Barges once called here to collect locally-produced salt, and to serve the local tide mill. Today, yachts dominate the scene, while visitors to the popular pub can dream of past glories as they look across to the mouth of the River Hamble.

Right

High Street, Hythe in September

Busy Hythe has an attractive High Street offering peaceful shopping, free from the clamour of motor vehicles. A modern marina development provides a haven, while ferries shuttle across to Southampton's Town Quay from the end of Hythe Pier. Six hundred and forty metres in length, it is served by a quaint little electric railway. The ferry link almost makes Hythe a suburb of Southampton.

Previous pages

Tide mill and moorings at Ashlett Creek in September

Hythe Electric Railway

Left

The electric railway at Hythe Pier (built 1879) in September

Originally the trucks on this railway were hand propelled and designed for the transport of goods. In 1922 the electrified track was laid to a 2ft 0in (610mm) gauge. The power is transmitted by means of a third rail on the seaward side of the track. The service is now powered by two four-wheel electric locomotives. Hythe Pier stretches 700 yards (640m) from the centre of Hythe to the deep water channel of Southampton Water. It is approximately 16 feet (5m) wide, and carries a pedestrian walkway and cycleway on its northern side, and the track of the Hythe Pier Railway on its southern side. Construction of the current pier started in 1879 and it was opened in 1881.

The Pier Railway is synchronised to the arrival and departure of the Hythe ferry. The service takes both passengers and bicycles on the 10 minute crossing to the Southampton side. Fine views of the *Queen Mary 2* and other ocean liners can be had from the Pier when they are in port.

Above

Wasp spider (female) at Hythe in August

This female wasp spider is one the many interesting and unusual examples of wildlife to be found in the area. The adult female is much larger than the male and can be twice the size. They are not dangerous to humans.

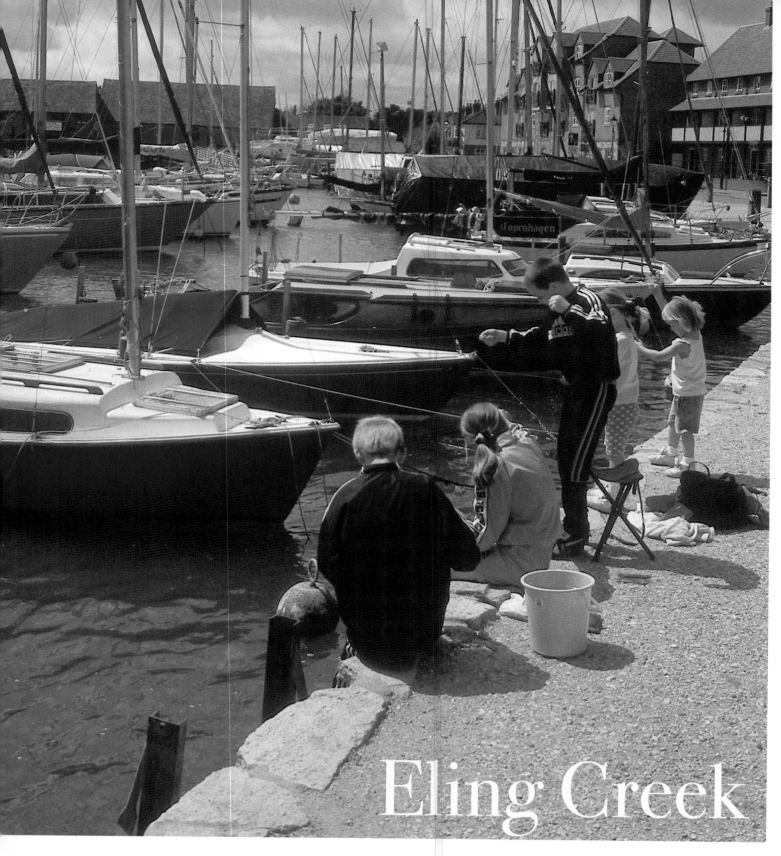

Eling Creek

Left

Eling Creek in July

Eling Creek is situated at the head of Southampton Water.
There is a Heritage Centre where visitors can learn about
the history of the area from the Bronze Age to the present
day. Eling Quay has been used as an active harbour for
hundreds of years. Tall-masted ships once unloaded their
goods here, and even today the industrial wharf is sometimes
used for commercial cargoes. The space is also shared by
fishermen and leisure yachtsmen sailing in Southampton
Water.

Above

Machinery at Eling Tide Mill in September

The sole remaining operational tide mill in the UK is situated
at Eling on an artificial causeway. The pair of independently
operated waterwheels drive a millstone each. To produce
good quality flour the tide has to be below the bottom of
the waterwheel for the mill to run efficiently. The waterwheels run on the outflow of the pond, not as is sometimes
said on the ebb tide. One of the wheels is kept as a static
exhibit to show the mechanism that would not be visible
when the wheel is moving.

Bartley Water

Above

The toll bridge at Eling in June

Left

Bartley Water estuary, Eling in August

This peaceful backwater straddles tiny Bartley Water as it spills into the River Test. Eling is guaranteed serenity by a toll bridge that acts as an effective buffer between it and the adjacent village of Totton. Once the centre of the large parish of Totton, Eling's rural setting on a hill overlooking Southampton Water is enhanced by Eling Creek and its causeway. Bartley Water is a stream flowing out into Southampton Water. Nearby the Redbridge Lower Test Nature Reserve supports typical species such as English Scurvy Grass, Sea Aster, Sea Arrowgrass and Wild Celery, whilst the brackish grassland has colonies of Hairy Buttercup, Brookweed and a rare grass known as the Bulbous Foxtail. At approximately 65-75 acres, the reed beds are one of the largest on the south coast.

Above

Redbridge Lower Test Nature Reserve, Totton in October

Southampton Docks

Right

Queen Mary 2 *docked at Southampton in January*

The bridge carrying the busy Waterloo to Bournemouth railway defines the head of Southampton Water. From this point you can head back to the Solent proper down its eastern side. The massive container docks and lines of vehicles for export – reminders of Southampton's raison d'etre – provide a dramatic introduction to the city itself. The days of great ocean liners and the special boat trains that spirited their passengers down from London are long gone, but an echo lingers in the shape of the many glitzy cruise liners that berth here.

Below

Vehicle export from Southampton in April

Tall Ships in Southampton

Left
Dar Mlodziezy, *a Polish training ship in Southampton Water*

The *Dar Mlodziezy,* which means 'Gift of Youth', is a steel-built Polish training ship. Although she looks as if she might be from an earlier age, she was in fact commisioned in 1982 to replace the famous *Dar Pomorza* 'Gift of Pomerania', which was built in 1909, as a training ship for the German Merchant Marine. *Dar Mlodziezy* was designed by the Polish naval architect Zygmunt Choren. A fully rigged 360-foot sailing ship, she was funded in the 1960s and 1970s by contributions from elementary school children. Her home port is Gdynia in Poland.

Above right.
Stavros S Niarchos, *a Sail Training Association ship in Southampton Water*

The *Stavros S Niarchos* is a British brig-rigged vessel with square sails on both masts. She normally sails with a crew of up to 67 people: a permanent salaried crew of 6, 11-13 volunteers and 48 voyage crew members. She is part of the Tall Ships Youth Trust, primarily designed to help young people develop character and purpose. She sometimes also sails with paying adult passengers which helps subsidise the expensive operation of a complex vessel of this type.

Above
Disney Wonder *in Southampton in July*

In complete contrast the *Disney Wonder* is a cruise ship built for 2,400 passengers and a crew of 1,000. She was refurbished in1999. Her gross tonnage is 83,000.

Above

Tudor Merchant's Hall and West Gate, Southampton in July

Although wartime bombing took its toll, enough old buildings and remnants of the city walls survive to remind us of its prosperous medieval origins. Southampton is said to have started when the Romans built a town called Clausentum. Since then Southampton has had a vigorous history.

The early buildings were built of wood, but when the merchants became wealthy they rebuilt their houses in stone.

During the Middle Ages a shipbuilding industry was created near the West Quay. Henry V's army sailed for the Battle of Agincourt from here in 1415. And in 1620 the Pilgrim Fathers departed in the *Speedwell* and the *Mayflower* having no idea that they would be making an unscheduled stop in Plymouth.

The Historic Old Town

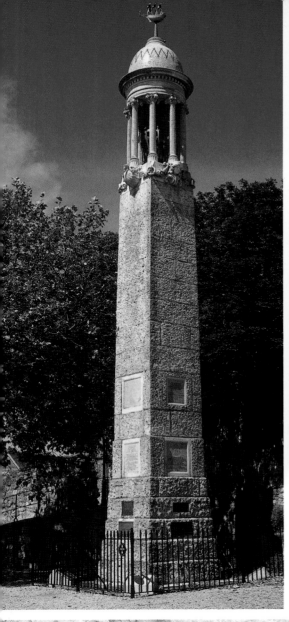

Left and below

The Pilgrim Fathers memorial in Southampton in June

The Leiden Separatists bought the ship *Speedwell* in Holland, and boarded it at Delftshaven. They then sailed to Southampton to meet the *Mayflower*, which had been chartered by the merchant investors. In Southampton they joined with other Separatists and the additional colonists hired by the investors.

The two ships began the voyage, but the *Speedwell* leaked so badly that the expedition had to return to England, first to Dartmouth and then to Plymouth. Finally, the Pilgrims sold the *Speedwell* and had to set out from Plymouth, on board the *Mayflower* alone.

Above left

Town walls, and cargo vessel replica

Above right

St Michael's Church spire through the town walls of Southampton

St Michael's Church, seen here through the town walls, was originally cross shaped. Building started in around 1070. The Norman tower still remains, it has rounded arches and was built using massive blocks of stone. There have been many changes but it still serves the people of Southampton even after 900 years.

THE PILGRIM FATHERS MEMORIAL SOUTHAMPTON. HAMPSHIRE. ENGLAND.
THE SEPARATIST CONGREGATION FROM BABWORTH, NOTTINGHAMSHIRE (1586-1604), WHICH MOVED TO SCROOBY IN 1606, TO AMSTERDAM, NETHERLANDS, IN 1608, AND TO LEYDEN IN 1609, SAILED FROM DELFT HAVEN IN THE SPEEDWELL ON AUGUST 1 (NEW STYLE), 1620, TO JOIN THE MAYFLOWER WITH ITS LONDON COLONISTS HERE. BOTH SHIPS SAILED ON AUGUST 15 (N.S.), 1620, FOR THE NEW WORLD. AFTER TURNING BACK TO DARTMOUTH, AND A SECOND TIME TO PLYMOUTH FOR REPAIRS, THE SPEEDWELL WAS ABANDONED, AND ON SEPTEMBER 16 (N.S.) THE MAYFLOWER ALONE SAILED TO PLYMOUTH, NEW ENGLAND, WITH 102 PASSENGERS.

THE GENERAL SOCIETY OF MAYFLOWER DESCENDANTS (U.S.A., 1897)
WALDO MORGAN ALLEN GOVERNOR GENERAL
ON THEIR FIRST PILGRIMAGE - 152 BY PLANES - TO THE NETHERLANDS AND ENGLAND
SEPTEMBER 22 - OCTOBER 6, 1955
335 YEARS AFTER THE SAILING OF THE MAYFLOWER

Above and right
Netley Abbey ruins in August

Beyond the mouth of the
River Itchen lies Netley
Abbey. Founded in 1239
by Peter des Roches, the
Bishop of Winchester from
1205–1238, it was dissolved
300 years later. All that
remains today are these
romantic ruins.

Right
*The Hospital Chapel (1856)
at Royal Victoria Country Park,
Netley in August*

South of Netley village is the
Royal Victoria Country Park,
the site of a hospital caring
for casualties of the Crimean
War. It, too, has been swept
away and only the imposing
chapel still stands.

Netley

Hamble River

Above

Crabbing at the Hamble River in June

The River Hamble rises near Bishop's Waltham and after 7.5 miles enters Southampton Water at Hamble-le-Rice. It is tidal and navigable up to Botley. The river provides many leisure opportunities for young and old alike, from boating to fishing for harbour crabs.

Right

Foxer Class yachts on the Hamble River in June

Foxer class dinghies are raced on the River Hamble at Warsash. Unlike the many competitive singlehanded dinghy classes, Foxer crews are not allowed to sit outside of the boat while racing. The distinctive red, black and white striped sails make for a colourful sight on many weekends.

Above and right

The Hamble to Warsash ferry in June

Warsash began as a small timber and fishing port at the mouth of the River Hamble, and also a landing-place for the Hamble to Warsash ferry – an important link in an historic route between Portsmouth and Southampton. The passenger ferry service between Hamble-le-Rice and Warsash operates between Hamble foreshore and Warsash (9am to 5.15pm weekdays, 9am to 5pm weekends, with extended operating times during the summer). The ferry operates on demand and can carry a maximum of 12 passengers at one time.

The earliest evidence of a crossing appears in a reference made at a local Admiralty Court in 1493. In 1508 comment was made as to the poor condition of the Warsash causeway. The men of Warsash were commanded to make suitable repairs.

Warsash Ferry

The black and white Harbour Master's Office at Warsash is a visually striking building, looking very much like a lighthouse.

A little way upstream is a colourful marina at Bursledon. A marvellous view can be obtained from the train as it crosses the Hamble on the way from Southampton to Portsmouth.

Before the end of the 18th Century, Warsash was probably a small community of fishermen's houses, farms and squatters' cottages built around the edge of the vast common which stretched to Swanwick in the north and to Titchfield in the east. It saw its fair share of smuggling as well as fishing, as is confirmed by numerous stories told by old families.

Warsash

3. Portsmouth Harbour

From Warsash, the north shore of the Solent is regained, and can be followed past Titchfield Haven National Nature Reserve and through the seaside centres of Hill Head and Lee-on-Solent to the town of Gosport on the western side of Portsmouth Harbour. Here the Gosport Ferry is used to cross to Portsmouth Harbour Railway Station in the centre of the naval city of Portsmouth.

HMS WARRIOR I

Above
Titchfield Haven Nature Reserve in November

This photograph captures the curiously shaved appearance
of the reed beds, their dense and tightly packed structure
providing a crisp edge to the water.

The reed beds are a nationally important habitat. They
attract Reed Warblers, Bearded Tits, Water Rails and Bittern.
They need to be cut and cleared in rotation to meet the
needs of the different species that make this place home.
Titchfield Haven is noted for being a glorious wetland and
reed bed nature reserve that extends across more than 140
hectares of the lower Meon Valley. It is a nationally renowned
reserve providing a winter refuge for a large variety of ducks,
geese and wading birds, as well as a summer breeding
ground for the rare Avocet.

Right
Fishing at Titchfield Haven in February

Titchfield was one of the major ports on the south coast in
early medieval times, being in a secure position on the River
Meon. Now, however, the river serves little purpose other
than as a place for a quiet spot of fishing on an early
February morning.

Previous pages
HMS Warrior, *Portsmouth in January*

Titchfield Haven

Above
Fort Brockhurst, Gosport in October

This monolithic entrance, with its menace emphasised
by the black water, offers no comfort to an unfortunate
internee or prospective invader. Brockhurst Fort in Gosport
is one of a number built in the 1860s to protect Portsmouth
and its vital harbour. Largely unaltered, the parade ground,
gun ramps and moated keep can all be viewed. The fort
currently stores a treasure trove of objects from English
Heritage's extensive reserve collections. Objects on display
have been excavated from sites in the South East and South
West and include stonework, textiles, jewellery, and furniture
from many periods. Photographed in the cold sun of
October a shiver might be felt at the prospect of an
enforced stay within its walls.

Gosport and Lee-on-Solent

Above

The seafront, Lee-on-Solent in October

Although seen at the same October time of year, this scene, with a clear blue sky and sharp shadows, offers a brisk afternoon stroll for the residents of Lee-on-Solent. The Victorian and Edwardian housing reflects the location's status as a popular resort just over a century ago. Meanwhile, the clatter of helicopters from HMS *Daedalus* tell of the airfield's switch from Fleet Air Arm base to a focus for air-sea rescue and police support aircraft. In view of the Solent's association with hovercraft technology, it is appropriate that a museum dedicated to their development has also been established here.

Portchester Castle

Above and left

Portchester Castle Re-enactment Society

A charming almost toy-like arrangement; a castle by the sea.
The small boats echo the thought, but do not be fooled.
Portchester Castle is a real medieval castle and former Roman
fort. It occupies a commanding position at the head of
Portsmouth Harbour. King Henry I founded the medieval
castle around 1120 as a defence against invasion. The site is
now owned by the state and managed by English Heritage.
Today it provides a dramatic stage for colourful re-enactments
drawn from its 2,000 year history.

Above
Portchester Castle in September

Here is another view in the September sun of the imposing Portchester Castle, near to Port Solent Marina. Anglo Saxon, within Roman walls, with Norman additions, it was captured by the French from King John in 1215 during the Barons' Rebellion – when they forced him to sign the Magna Carta. Richard II turned part of it into a palace in 1396 after the Hundred Years War with France, and Henry V left for Agincourt from its ramparts. It housed troops during the English Civil War in the 17th century and prisoners of the Napoleonic wars in the 18th.

There is an Augustinian priory chapel that was built before the castle fell into Royal hands; 18th and 19th century graffiti on the walls from the French prisoners, as well as extensive archaeological finds from the Roman and Anglo Saxon era can be seen here.

Right
Children sail training off Portchester in September

Portchester Lake provide excellent shelter for youngsters to learn to sail. The Portchester Sailing Club, close to the castle, has several hundred members, with sections for cruisers and dinghies. The children can practice an intentional capsize in the shallow water here.

Sail Training

The sheer size of this weapon of mass destruction is intimidating. The scale of the ship can be appreciated if two members of the *Ark Royal's* crew are spotted to the left of the main superstructure. In this friendly September sunshine perhaps it is difficult to imagine the ship at war, with military aircraft launching themselves off the strongly canted deck, accompanied by the ships' guns blazing at the enemy with protective ferocity.

Portsmouth has been synonymous with the Royal Navy since the end of the 15th century. Britain's three aircraft carriers, HMS *Ark Royal,* HMS *Illustrious* and HMS *Invincible* are based here, as well as a fleet of destroyers, frigates, mine warfare ships and offshore patrol vessels.

A harbour tour takes 45 minutes and enables visitors to enjoy fascinating views whilst listening to a lively commentary. Founded in 1911, the Royal Naval Museum is one of country's leading maritime museums and is the only museum devoted to the ships of the Royal Navy and the men and women who served on them. Visitors can see, touch, hear and even smell the history of the Royal Navy through a rich collection of artefacts and award-winning permanent exhibitions.

Portsmouth is also the birthplace of Isambard Kingdom Brunel and Charles Dickens. Today, it offers new and exciting developments, as well as being a seaside resort, water sports and wildlife habitat.

Below
Once upon a time, only sailors had a tattoo; nowadays it is popular among many young people

Portsmouth Dockyard

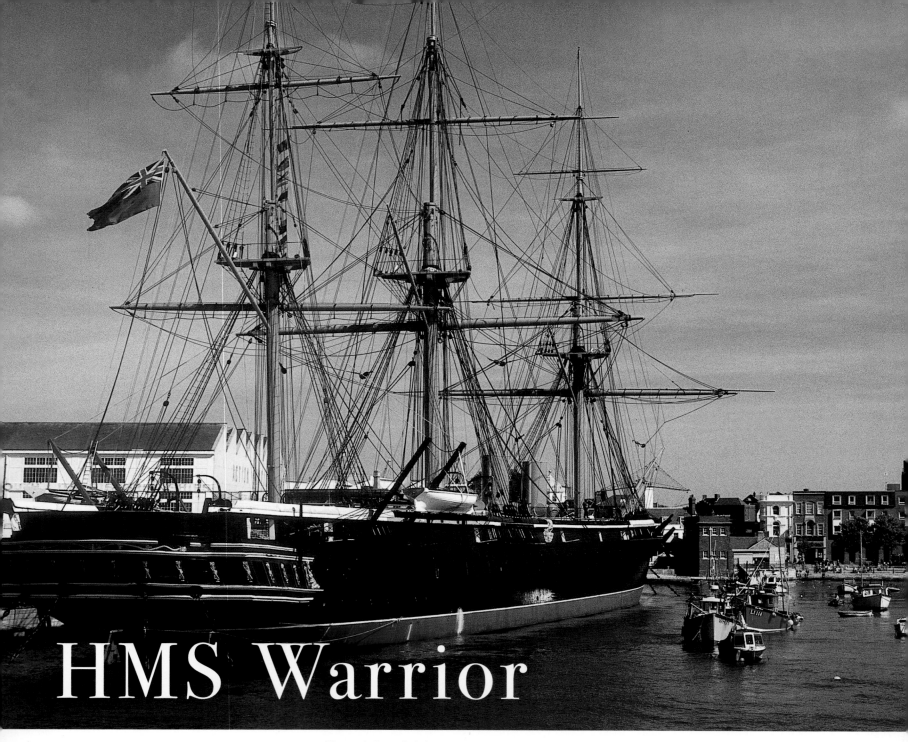

HMS Warrior

Above, left and right
HMS Warrior at Portsmouth in September

After the ships of the Royal Navy it is to the old dockyard that many of Portsmouth's visitors are drawn, and with good reason: the *Mary Rose,* HMS *Victory* and HMS *Warrior* are representatives of naval excellence dating from the 15th, 18th and 19th centuries respectively. When completed in October 1861, HMS *Warrior* was by far the largest, fastest, most heavily-armed and most heavily-armoured warship the world had ever seen. HMS *Warrior* was saved from being scrapped by the Maritime Trust. As the world's first iron-hulled battleship, she was recognised as one of the Royal Navy's most historically important warships.

HMS Victory

Far left.
HMS Victory, *Portsmouth*

Two figureheads, the man and his ship, perhaps two of the most iconic symbols of our maritime history.

On 12 January 1922 HMS *Victory* was moved into the oldest drydock in the world, No. 2 dock at Portsmouth, for restoration. In 1928 King George V was able to unveil a tablet celebrating the completion of the work, although restoration work and maintenance was still to continue under the supervision of the Society for Nautical Research.

Over the last few years the ship has undergone another very extensive restoration to bring her appearance as close as possible to that which she had at Trafalgar, for the bicentenary of the battle in October 2005. Replicas of items including mess bowls, beakers and tankards in the 'Marine's Mess', and a toothbrush, shaving brush and wash bowl in 'Hardy's Cabin' are on display.

Left
The Nelson Statue at Southsea Common

This statue is a reminder of Nelson's famous signal, 'England expects that every man will do his duty'.

Above and right
Gunwharf Quays, Portsmouth in September

A very different scene from the ships of war. Fast catamaran ferries to Ryde leave from the jetty adjacent to Portsmouth Harbour station, while next door is Gunwharf Quays, once the Royal Navy's principal ordnance depot and, later, a torpedo school. It is now a cornucopia of retail outlets, bars and restaurants. Visitors wander through Old Portsmouth to discover nearby the cathedral serving a parish of 5,000 and a diocese of many thousands more. This haven of spirituality in a busy city can trace its origins back to the 12th century.

This waterfront overlooks the Gunwharf Quays Marina which has hosted many national and international sailing events. When not in the media spotlight, the marina accommodates luxurious multi-million pound superyachts and famous tall ships from around the globe.

Gunwharf Quays

Spinnaker Tower

Soaring above everything is a potent symbol of a Portsmouth reborn – the glittering Spinnaker Tower. Clarence Pier is also pregnant with symbolism. It represents the watershed between the bustle of Portsmouth and Southsea's summer playground. Not only does it host the terminal for hovercraft that zip across to Ryde in minutes, but it also marks the way to 16th century Southsea Castle and tangible reminders of a more recent conflict: the D-Day Museum and the statue of Viscount Montgomery.

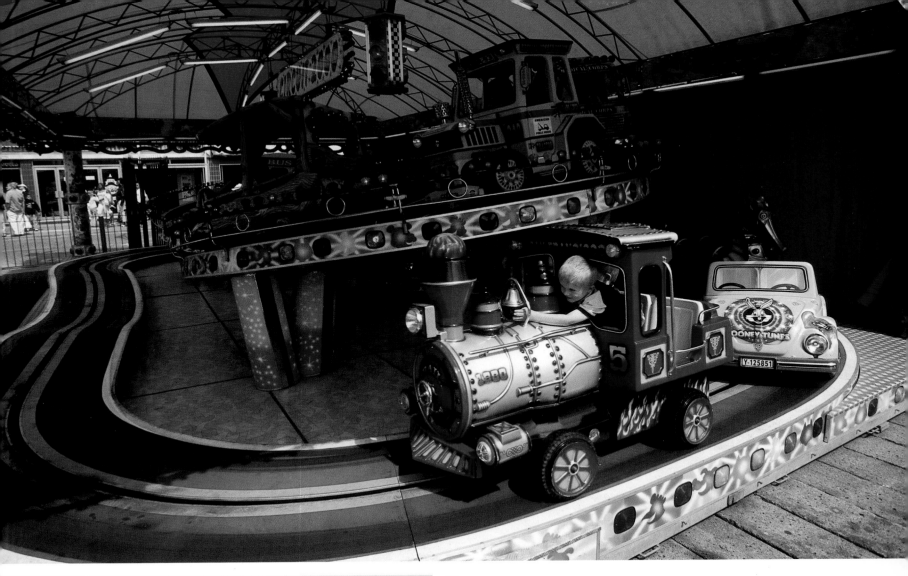

Above

The funfair at Southsea in June

The Southsea beach has two piers: South Parade Pier and Clarence Pier. Both house amusement arcades; South Parade Pier also has a ballroom and a bar area. Clarence Pier is adjacent to a permanent funfair.

Left

Yellow Horned Poppy at Southsea in June

The Yellow Horned Poppy on Southsea beach is a typical colonising plant of bare shingle. The plants flower from their second year onwards and live for between 2 and 5 years. Although the large and beautiful yellow flowers generally only last a day, flowering starts in mid-May. Seen here in June they may still be appearing well into October.

A Ferry to France

The obvious excitement of a trip to France can be sensed from the crowds lining the decks. This monumental slab of steel may not achieve elegance but the sheer scale is breathtaking when up close like this.

Portsmouth is the second best known port in the United Kingdom after Dover. In a central position on the South coast of England, Portsmouth is a busy ferry port taking passengers to destinations such as Caen, St Malo, Cherbourg and Le Havre in France, and Bilbao in Spain. As many as 3.4 million people travel through the ferry port every year.

Portsmouth Harbour also has passenger ferry links to Gosport and the Isle of Wight. Britain's longest-standing commercial hovercraft service, begun in the 1960s, still runs from near Clarence Pier to Ryde, Isle of Wight.

4. Chichester Harbour

Our route now follows the northern shores of Langstone Harbour past Farlington Marsh Nature Reserve to the village of Langstone. From Langstone the path follows the north coast of Chichester Harbour and passes Bosham, Itchenor, and Wittering, before reaching its end at the village of Selsey.

Above
Farlington Marshes Nature Reserve in December

To the north east and jutting out into Langstone Harbour are Farlington Marshes. Originally unenclosed salt marsh and mudflats, it is now a wildflower-rich grazing marsh, internationally important for migratory birds, particularly the Brent Goose, Black-tailed Godwit, Wigeon, Teal, Shoveler, Pintail and other ducks, Curlew, Dunlin and Redshank. Raptors are also common, and Short Eared Owls, Peregrine, Kestrels and others can be seen in season. This precious nature reserve is within minutes of the city centre. Winter need not be dull when this landscape is on the doorstep.

Right
Brent Geese at Farlington Marshes in December

Farlington Marshes

Above

Bird watchers at Farlington Marshes in January

The Solent has a large number of outstanding birdwatching habitats, including ancient woodlands, chalk grassland, lowland heath, river valleys, lakes, reedbeds, coastal grazing marshes and intertidal mudflats. The only habitats it lacks are uplands and cliffs. There are many bird watching organisations who monitor the reserves in the area. Farlington Marshes are particularly noteworthy for scarce migrants.

Right

Brent Geese in flight at Farlington Marshes in December

Brent Geese flocks follow each other in impressive formation.

Bird Watching

Above and right

Fishermen's cottages and The Royal Oak at Langstone

South of Havant, these picturesque cottages and a comfortable inn at Langstone look out over the water to Hayling Island, dreaming perhaps of the village's transition from smugglers' haunt to sailing centre. The harbour frontage features the Old Mill, The Royal Oak public house and some fishermen's cottages, which have almost become the Borough 'trademark' so often are they drawn, photographed or painted. The village was formerly the Port of Havant and had its own customs officials. As late as the end of the 19th century it was a coasting port and at one time a train ferry service ran from Langstone to St Helens on the Isle of Wight. It is a well-known sailing centre with good moorings and Langstone Sailing Club has its headquarters here.

The nucleus of the village has been designated as a conservation area. From the Old Mill a path runs eastwards along the shore to Warblington and Emsworth, although part can be covered by very high tides.

Langstone

Above
South Street, Emsworth in June

South Street Emsworth. A view over water, the perfect
end to a street. These simple houses reveal their history in
the clearly defined brick additions to the original rough stone
buildings.

Chichester Harbour comprises four gnarled fingers:
the Emsworth, Thorney, Bosham and Chichester channels.
Collectively, they enjoy a range of national and international
designations to protect their unique habitats and wildlife,
particularly the significant numbers of breeding and migratory
water birds. A railway line runs virtually arrow-straight for
eight miles from Emsworth to Chichester. The Harbour's
shoreline, on the other hand, meanders for some 50 miles
in total, most of this being protected by sea walls that
offer good walks.

Right
The waterfront at Emsworth in September

Transporting stores past the flood defence wall separating
the houses from the sea.

Emsworth

Emsworth Waterfront

Above

Common Sea Lavender at Bosham in June

The erect oval leaves of this plant, the Common Sea Lavender, have glands on the surface which it uses to discharge the salt it naturally gathers from the harsh saline environment. Many species flourish in saline soils, and are therefore common near coasts and in salt marshes.

Some variants have been used as decorative dry flowers. The lavender colour gives the plant its name, although there the resemblance stops as there is none of the distinctive smell associated with the Common Lavender (*Lavandula Angustifolia*). Colours can range from pink to violet and purple. They are popular with butterflies, bees and other insects for their nectar.

Above

Dinghy and swans at Emsworth in September

There are at least fifteen sailing clubs, several marinas
and over 10,000 boats in Chichester Harbour, providing
employment for many local people engaged in boat building,
sail making and chandlery. This picture was taken at low tide.

Above

Bayeux tapestry extract at Bosham Church in June

Bosham is the only church shown on the Bayeux Tapestry. It depicts the chancel arch. Harold, Earl of Wessex inherited the Manor and Church of Bosham from his father Earl Godwin. King Harold set sail from Bosham in 1064 to discuss the future of the throne of England after the death of Edward the Confessor. Harold's sister was the wife of Edward, so self interest prevailed and Harold was crowned King, much to to the dismay of William. Later, when Harold was killed at the Battle of Hastings, William had his revenge and became King himself. He took over the manor and Church of Bosham as a royal domain. The Domesday Book of 1084 shows Bosham as one of the wealthiest English churches, its property totalling 13,000 acres spread over different parts of the country.

Left

Bosham Church in June

Bosham Church of the Holy Trinity is largely Saxon. This picture illustrates the quiet setting amidst the cemetery and surrounding trees. Bosham is said to be the oldest Christian site in Sussex, thought to be built on a Roman site. Of the basilica, only the bases of the chancel arch pillars remain. The church building was probably begun during the reign of King Canute, who lived in Bosham, where his eight year old daughter is reputed to have died and been buried at the church. The site of the famous legend of Canute and the waves is claimed by many places along this coast, but Bosham with Canute's status as a resident could well give strength to the story.

Bosham

Above

Dinghy launching at Bosham in October

There are several sailing clubs in Bosham. They have the advantage of a beautiful setting, almost beyond perfect. This photograph shows a Mirror dinghy on the left and a Laser on the right, and sailing takes place all through the year. The Quay gives access to Bosham Channel at all states of the tide.

Tidal Bosham

Left
Low tide at Bosham in September

Given the wonderful location it is no surprise that sailing is a major activity here. Some people have bought homes in this area simply for that reason. Olympic medal winners such as Mark Covell sail and train on the water. There are about sixteen yacht clubs in Chichester Harbour, which is one of the best natural harbours in the UK. Not all is perfect though. The tides can sometimes make it difficult to sail as the currents can be strong and an unwanted stranding on the mud can spoil your day. Although not quite so serious for the dinghy sailor, an unwary keelboat crew can find themselves isolated and alone for several hours. The usually safe waters, though, are ideal for learning to sail.

Bosham has a vast foreshore where the unlucky motorist will find, as King Canute did, that the tide is not inclined to change its manners and will engulf any carelessly parked cars. There are several warning signs along Shore Road saying 'This road floods each tide'. The water frequently covers Shore Road in both summer and winter. It provides some amusement to locals who enjoy watching, and even collect photographs which are displayed on the walls of a local pub.

Right
Windsurfing at Sinah, Hayling Island in February

This photograph taken at Sinah in February shows why windsurfing was invented on Hayling Island. Originally it was thought to be an American invention, but after a court battle the title was given to Hayling Island.

West Beach is the designated windsurfing area of the Hayling seafront. This was introduced over ten years ago to help keep windsurfers and swimmers away from each other. The windsurfers are aware of the situation and take care when launching and landing. West Beach is also a popular spot for surfers and body boarders when the conditions are right.

Access is from Seafront Road, just west of the bottom of Staunton Avenue. The western fringe of the Island once hosted the tiny branchline train that shuttled down from Havant. It did good business during the summer, but in winter it slumbered. Closure came in 1966 and the trackbed has been converted for use by cyclists, horseriders and walkers. South Hayling is the principal focus of a popular holiday destination with the usual trappings associated with an extensive beach. These include a miniature railway and a golf course at Sinah, where this photograph was taken.

West Beach

Hayling Island

Left
Recovering Hayling Lifeboat, near Black Point, Hayling Island

Recovering the Hayling Lifeboat on a February day at Sandy Point, sometimes known as Black Point. Sandy Point is the south east tip of the Island. Since 1975, Sandy Point has also been the Hayling home of the RNLI, who have a station at this entrance to Chichester Harbour. Crewed by volunteers, and funded entirely through charitable donation, the lifeboats of Hayling are on standby throughout the year and serve to make the waters safer. For those wishing to see the boats up close, the boathouse is open to the public every Sunday, and they are launched on exercise every Wednesday.

Above
Geese, ducks and waders at the Kench Nature Reserve.
High tide at Sinah, Hayling Island in February

The Kench is a small naturally protected inter-tidal inlet close to the entrance to Langstone Harbour. Much of the Kench is now a local nature reserve run by Hampshire Council, who purchased it after a series of attempts to develop it as a marina had failed in the planning process. The whole of this inlet can be seen from Ferry Road and there is also a path up the east side taking you to the shore of Langstone Harbour.

Just north of the mouth of the Kench is a large shingle bank running north – the only remnant of an early attempt to construct a railway line, doomed to failure by the wind and waves in the harbour.

Above

The Crown and Anchor pub garden, at Dell Quay in September

The Crown and Anchor is an 18th century riverside pub located on the Chichester Estuary at Dell Quay. There are panoramic views of Chichester Harbour and as can be seen here, a three tier terraced garden going down to the sea.

Right

Richard Uttley, Dolphin Quay Boatyard, Emsworth in June

Dolphin Quay is one of the few yards left in the area that has experience working on classic wooden boats. Yachtsmen and tourists throng this ancient landing-place and Dell Quay is probably busier than it ever was in the past. Although there is no specific village centre, there are a number of marine related businesses and boatyards. The shipwright, Richard Uttley, is seen here restoring a wooden boat.

Dell Quay is the port of Chichester and also home to the Education Centre. In the early 1800s there were over a hundred ships registered here. Five hundred years earlier it was rated the 7th most important port in the Kingdom. Small coastal barges and local boats carried wool and grain to London and foreign ports, and brought back coal, timber and cargoes of anything needed for the City of Chichester.

Dell Quay

Above

The waterfront at Emsworth in September

Straddling the Hampshire-Sussex border is the small town of Emsworth. Its oyster industry may be no more, but local craftsmen are still engaged in boatbuilding. And in summer visitors flock to the waterfront with its forest of yacht masts and to enjoy the spectacle of colourful sails and the ever-present swans. The village itself is picturesque with narrow streets, Georgian houses, high walled gardens, and a good selection of village shops and restaurants. The pretty millponds are home to a variety of wildlife. A visit to this unique village is a must for all harbour lovers. Magnificent views to the downs, Hayling Island and Thorney Island are an added bonus. In winter migrating birds use this area as a temporary home.

The town has 11 pubs, many of which are in or within easy reach of the square with some dating back to the 18th century. The shopping area radiates out from the square and has the feel of old rural England with its range of specialist shops and locally-caught fish.

Right

Metal detecting at low tide at Dell Quay in September

In the 19th century almost every kind of trade was found in Emsworth: there were tailors, boot and shoemakers, and shopkeepers selling all kinds of goods. Today visitors can search the foreshore with metal detectors looking for lost treasure.

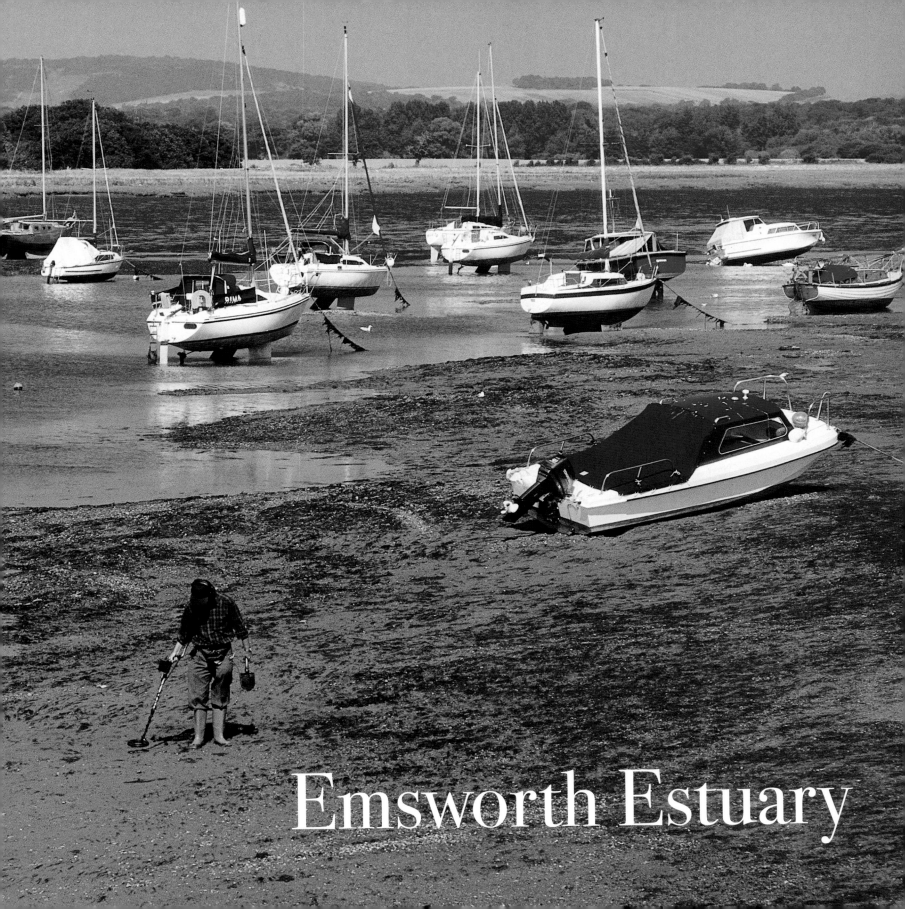

Emsworth Estuary

Above and right

Roman Villa mosaic at Fishbourne in May

Fishbourne Roman Palace was discovered by accident during the digging of a watermain trench in 1960. The discovery led to nine seasons of excavations that showed the site had developed from a military base at the time of the Roman invasion in AD43 to a sumptuous palace by the end of the first century. Between 1995 and 2002, new excavations by the Sussex Archaeological Society revealed exciting new insights into the development of this site, and especially the area in front of the Palace. Shown above is the Cupid on a Dolphin mosaic.

The Palace houses the largest collection of in-situ mosaic floors in Britain. Many of these were laid around AD75-80, which makes them some of the oldest mosaics in the country. The original palace had approximately 100 rooms, most of which had mosaic floors. Of these, just over a quarter survive to some degree, ranging from small, isolated patches to almost complete floors.

The earliest mosaics at Fishbourne tend to be black geometric patterns on a white background; something that was popular in Italy at the time. The designs may have arrived in pattern books and would have been adapted to suit local requirements. The mosaicists came from Italy, as there would have been none in Britain with the necessary expertise. The materials, however, were local. The white tesserae, or stone cubes, are of chalk and the dark grey of limestone.

Fishbourne Roman Palace

Chichester Channel

Left

Chichester Channel from Salterns Copse in May

The open stretch of water provides excellent sailing, which is popular early in the year, even though the ambient temperature isn't high. Place names reflect the history of an area, and in this case salt pans were located nearby.

Above

Chichester Channel, Itchenor in January

A view of Chichester Channel from Itchenor, which takes its name from the Saxon chieftain Icca who first resettled the district after the collapse of Roman Britain. The parish is still officially called West Itchenor, despite the fact that the village of East Itchenor disappeared in the 15th century. Around 1175 the then Lord of Itchenor built a chapel on the manor which developed into a parish church by the end of the century. The church is dedicated to St Nicholas, the patron saint of seamen, and has its own graveyard. During the 18th century there was a considerable amount of shipbuilding which lasted until the end of the Napoleonic wars.

A small boatbuilding presence is recorded throughout the years but permanent boatbuilding and repairs restarted with Haines' yard in 1912.

In the late 18th century the 3rd Duke of Richmond built Itchenor Lodge as his yachting home plus a salt-water bath on the shore near where the Conservancy Office now stands. His sloop, the *Goodwood,* was used to bring stone from various places for both the building of Itchenor House and Goodwood House.

By 1927 the yachtsmen and dinghy sailors of Itchenor had started their own sailing club. They acquired four small 17th century cottages which were converted to form their clubhouse. The original buildings have since been enlarged and improved. During the last war the club was requisitioned, first by the Army and then by the Navy, when preparing for the D-Day landings.

Today many of the inhabitants of Itchenor have bought homes in the village to enjoy the sailing. Midweek and during the winter the village is quiet, the only activity taking place around the boatyards, Harbour Office and pub. However, at weekends and during the summer holidays the village comes alive with visitors.

Above

Harbour front at Itchenor in October

Itchenor had, and still has, a tradition of shipbuilding. Small ships were built in Tudor times, which were paid for by the merchants of Chichester. The biggest ship ever built was 140ft (50m) long, and carried 44 cannons. She was launched in 1785.

There is a legend that when the Vikings came into the harbour, they rowed up to Bosham under the cover of fog. They raided the village, set fire to the wattle and daub houses, and stole the church bell. When the fog lifted, the men of Itchenor saw what had happened and were waiting for the long boat when it came down the creek. In the fight, the bell sank to the bottom. Afterwards they dredged the mud, but each time the grapnel brought the bell to the surface, the rope broke and the bell sank into the mud again.

So, the bell lies forever in Bell Hole, and if you listen on a quiet evening you might hear it ring.

Right

Winter boat cleaning at Itchenor in January

Itchenor

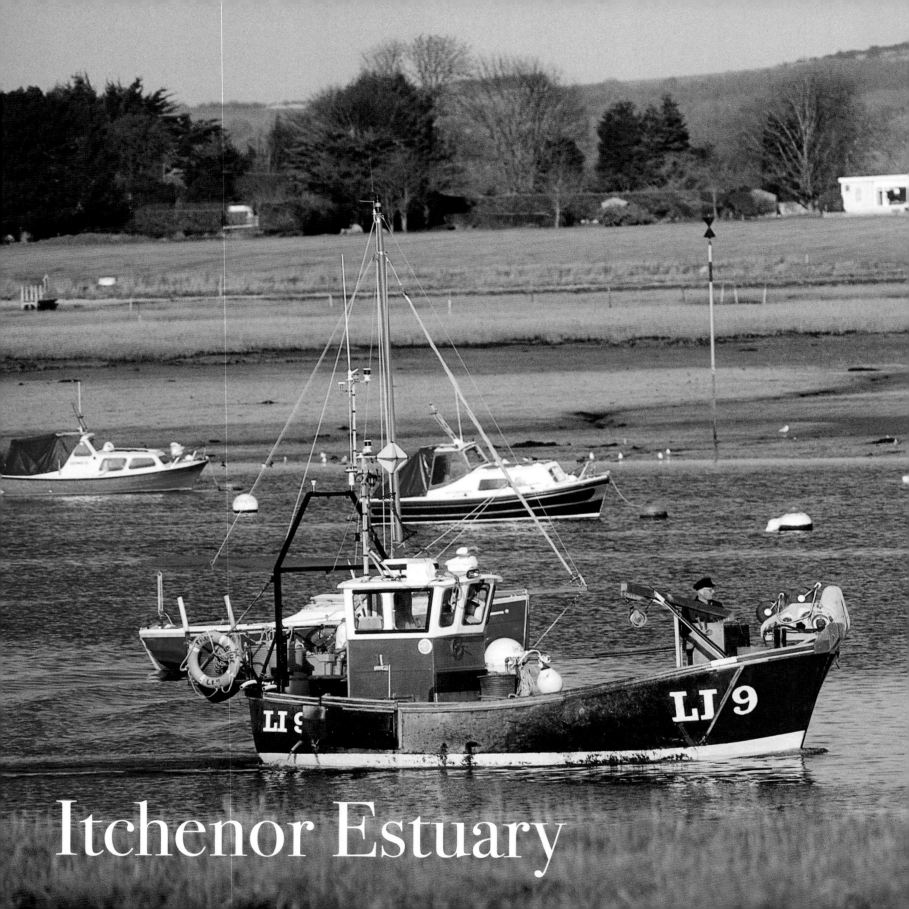

Itchenor Estuary

Above

St Nicholas, Church, Itchenor in April

The small but attractive church of St Nicholas is set on
a small hillock beside the road leading to the harbour.
Dating from the late 12th century, it is a rectangular building
only 50 feet long and 16 feet 6 inches wide, with no
structural division between the nave and chancel. The oldest
furnishing in the church is the octagonal font of the 13th
century, set on four subsidiary columns on a moulded
base. The roof, the stained glass and almost all the other
furnishings date from this century. All this work is of fine
quality and the beauty of the church has been much
enhanced.

Left

Fishermen returning to Itchenor in January

The various channels and creeks within Chichester Harbour
yield some quite surprising fish, such as the occasional plaice
or even sole. Many of these species have been caught in
recent years, some of them weighing in excess of two
pounds. Mackerel are sometimes caught inside the harbour
but more frequently outside, where bream and a variety of
other species give sport in season.

Chichester Canal

Above

Chichester Canal next to Chichester Marina in May

Construction started on the Chichester Canal by Act of
Parliament in 1819. Three years later (1822) it opened,
consisting of 2 locks and 6 bridges. The canal was 6km long
from Birdham at the seaward end to Chichester Basin, and its
principal trade was coal for the local gasworks. The canal never
carried the amount of goods first envisaged, and as with most
canals in Sussex it was abandoned in the period 1868-1875.
The Chichester city council took over its ownership in 1892 to
ensure Chichester's connection to the sea remained. In 1906
the last commercial cargo of six tons of shingle was carried
from Birdham to Chichester Basin.

Salterns Lock is the seaward lock from Chichester
Harbour and the entrance to the canal. It is in full working
order and is notable for one set of wooden lock gates at the
seaward end and cast iron gates at the canal side. Its main use
(infrequently) is for boats to reach a limited number of moorings along the first half mile of the canal.

Right

Nesting mute swan in the Chichester Canal in April

Nesting mute swans now take advantage of the peace and
quiet where once the clamour of industry held sway.

Birdham Pool

Left

The Old Mill and lock gates, Birdham Pool in September

At Birdham we find the splendid Old Mill and lock gates
for the entrance to a small marina that was originally the
millpond. Nearby are the lock gates of the disused
Chichester Canal. It may be that there was a watermill at
Birdham since the time of the Normans, but early 18th
century maps do not show one, and the present mill was
built in 1768. The rising tide was apparently allowed into the
pond, and on the ebb, after a good head of water had been
secured, the outgoing water turned the mill wheels. The
owners of the tide mills worked unusual hours as the tide
waits for no man! The mill ceased to grind corn in the 1930s
and lock gates were once again built into the wall of the mill
pond and the small yacht basin was developed.

Above

A cormorant at Birdham Pool in November

This cormorant obviously can't read. They are coastal rather
than oceanic birds, and some have colonised inland waters.
All are fish eaters, dining on small eels and fish. They dive
from the surface, though many species make a characteristic
half-jump as they dive, presumably to give themselves a more
streamlined entry into the water. Underwater they propel
themselves with their feet. After fishing they are frequently
seen holding their wings out in the sun; it is assumed that this
is to dry them. Unusually for a water bird, their feathers are
not waterproofed. This may help them dive quickly, since their
feathers do not retain air bubbles.

West Wittering

Left
*Windsurfing at
West Wittering in July*

The village of West Wittering
lies to the east of the entrance
to Chichester Harbour, behind
the sand spit of East Head.
Summer finds the village
thronged with visiting tourists
attracted by the beautiful
sandy beaches. A thriving
windsurfing club has also
grown up at West Wittering.

Since it stands at the
harbour mouth it seems quite
likely that the Romans founded
some kind of small coastal
defence here, and there were
certainly other fortifications in
later times. Over the years the
sea has given up a strange
variety of treasures, ranging
from the flotsam of broken
ships to their cannons and
anchors and other valuable
cargoes. Can all the wine and
brandy washed ashore really
have come from sunken
vessels? Amongst the clever
deceits of the smugglers was
the trick of allowing the tide to
land their wares.

Over the centuries much
land has been washed away
into the sea. The effects of
coastal erosion are still felt at
East Head, which is under
constant threat.

Right
Sand Art Day at East Head, West Wittering in July

For several years the Chichester Harbour Conservancy organised a Sand Art Day on the beach at East Head. Some constructed sculptures of crocodiles, ships or mermaids, some drew patterns, some made castles in the sand. Although families can still enjoy a day on the beach the organised event will not take place in the future due to concerns about beach conservation. The Harbour Conservancy, however, has many plans for other events to come.

Above and left
Erosion defences at East Head sand dunes in September

The sand dune spit is about 1,000 metres long and 400 metres wide at the widest point and covers about 10 hectares. It is joined to the mainland by a very narrow strip at the car park end which is known as the 'hinge'. The sea broke through at this point in October 2004, but the effect of the breach is being mitigated by the sand and shingle recharge, which was positioned in 2005. The beach on the western (seaward) side is mostly fine sand with shingle at the northern end, and East Head has been formed from this sand washed along the coast from east to west by a process known as longshore drift. The sand is deposited on the shallow area on the seaward side of the feature, which at low tide can be dried and blown by the wind onto the shore to form the dunes.,

East Head

Above

The village centre of Selsey in April

The village of Selsey sits at the end of Selsey Bill peninsula and it is possible to hear the sea on three sides from the centre of the village which lies some half mile north of the most southern point. The derivation of the name 'Selsey' is popularly considered to be Seal Island. There is no doubt that until the end of the 18th century, the peninsula was an island with its own ferry, ferryhouse and ferryman, who was paid 'four bushels of barley in 1661 and allowed to collect a half-penny from every traveller'. The causeway was completed in 1809. Selsey was once an isolated fishing community, with 3 Coastguard Stations and a Lloyds of London semaphore signal station. Long established, it is probable that a mint existed at Selsey prior to Roman times. By the 20th century Selsey had become an oasis for writers, musicians and authors.

Selsey Bill

Above
The Lifeboat Station at Selsey in January

In 1838, even before a lifeboat was stationed at Selsey, a Silver Medal was awarded to Lieut. E B Westbrook RN for saving three men from the sloop *Ann*.

Before an RNLI Lifeboat Station was established in 1861 many rescues took place off the coast. A double-banked lifeboat, named *Friend* (35 feet long with 12 rowing oars) was later sent to the station, the cost of which was provided for by the Society of Friends. This lifeboat was launched over the beach on skids.

Selsey Crabs and Lobsters

Left

Bringing in the catch at Selsey in January

The Selsey fishing fleet consists of 14 vessels. They fish for lobster, crab and whelk, and the fleet moors in the area close to the Lifeboat Station. The Selsey fishermen's organisation has taken a lead in introducing undersized lobster escape hatches which allow the smaller ones to crawl out, thereby helping to conserve stocks and allow the youngsters to grow to full size. Some unwanted scraps thrown overboard from the fishing boats assist in attracting the abundance of marine life that can be found in the area.

Above

Unloading the whelk catch at Selsey in January

5. The Isle of Wight

The Isle of Wight has a wonderfully unspoilt coastline from the famous Needles rocks to the multi-coloured sandstone of Alum Bay. There are two stretches of 'Heritage Coast' which cover nearly half of the island's 60 mile (97km) coastline. Within an area of just 147 square miles (3,800 hectares) over 500 miles of carefully maintained and well signposted rights of way can be found. Thatched cottages, ancient churches and manor houses, can be found in leafy lanes winding their way from coast to coast.

The towns and villages hold special interest because their historic buildings have been relatively untouched by the fashions and trends on mainland Britain. Queen Victoria and Prince Albert established a favourite residence at Osborne, and their names are reflected throughout the island.

Right
Needles Park chairlift, Alum Bay

An amusement park exists at the top of the Needles cliffs, and during the summer season a chairlift takes tourists down to the beach below. The Needles Park chairlift continues to be a firm favourite with visitors and it is the best way to see the Isle of Wight's most famous landmark. Take a ride in one of the 50 chairs from the top of the cliff to Alum Bay Beach and back. The views are truly spectacular, from the picturesque Needles Rocks and lighthouse to the multi-coloured sand cliffs.

Needles Lift

Alum Bay

Right
The cliffs and coloured sands at Alum Bay in September

Alum Bay is a sandy bay near the westernmost point of
the Isle of Wight, within sight of The Needles. The bay is
particularly noted for its multi-coloured sand cliffs.

Samples of the sand in vials and jars were for many
years available in tourist shops all over the island. Some fine
examples of pictures made with the coloured sand also exist.
The days are gone when ordinary people could dig out their
own sands, and signs on the beach warn tourists not to climb
the cliffs because of the danger of sandslides.

Most Islanders are aware that Alum Bay gets its name
from some sort of mineral located there. Surprisingly the
alum seam has never been identified, and there is no record
of it actually being mined.

Above
Totland Bay on a quiet day in October

Totland Bay is stuated on the west side of the Island, where
families can enjoy the delightful beach. The resort has sprung
into prominence and grown very fast during the last few
years. Many of the houses are quite picturesque. There is a
pier, and during summer a regular service of boats from
Lymington, as well as excursion traffic. The beach is steep,
so visitors can bathe at any state of the tide.

Albert and Victoria Forts

Above
The Solent from Fort Victoria in September

Named after Queen Victoria (1846-1901) who first visited the Isle of Wight as a princess in 1831, this was the beginning of a 70-year association with the island. Queen Victoria and Prince Albert began to spend more of their time on the island in 1864 and the Prince then set about redesigning and rebuilding Osborne House.

Left
The Solent's western entrance from Fort Albert

Fort Albert is a tower fort nestling under the cliffs west of Fort Victoria near Yarmouth. It was also known as Cliff End Fort, named after the northern extremity of Colwell Bay. Fort Albert was one of the Royal Commission forts built in the 19th century as part of Lord Palmerston's defences against the possibility of a French attack from Napoleon III. Designed to defend the Needles Passage, it was completed in 1856, after 4 years of construction. With the introduction of armoured ships the fort was obsolete by 1858.

Hurst Castle

Above

Hurst Castle from Fort Albert in September

Fort Albert was built to guard the Western Solent at a time when invasion by the French was a very real threat. It was the centrepiece in a ring of massive fortifications constructed to protect the Isle of Wight and the strategic naval base at Portsmouth. The design was said to have been conceived by Prince Albert himself.

Hurst Castle is one of Henry VIII's Device Forts, built at the end of a long shingle spit at the west end of the Solent to guard the approaches to Portsmouth. It was sited at the narrow entrance to the Solent where the ebb and flow of the tides creates strong currents, putting would-be invaders at its mercy.

Charles I was imprisoned here in 1648 before being taken to London for his trial and execution. The castle was given extensive new wing batteries after the 1859 Royal Commission report, and the modifications were completed in 1873. During World War II, Hurst was manned with coastal gun batteries and searchlights. The castle is now owned by English Heritage and is open to the public.

Right

The Harbour, Yarmouth in May

Situated on the estuary of the western River Yar, picturesque Yarmouth Harbour has berthing and on-shore facilities for visiting yachtsmen. A ferry service operates from Lymington to Yarmouth. The cycleway to Freshwater follows the route of the former railway line, so that walkers, cyclists and birdwatchers can also enjoy the riverside trails. Yarmouth has some excellent small shops, cafés, restaurants and traditional pubs.

Yarmouth has been a settlement for over a thousand years, and is one of the very earliest on the Isle of Wight. The first record of a settlement here was in King Ethelred the Unready's record of the Danegeld tax of 991. It was originally called Eremue, meaning 'muddy estuary'. The Normans laid out the streets of Yarmouth on the grid system, a plan which can still be seen in the layout today. It grew rapidly, and was given its first Charter as a town in 1135. The town became a parliamentary borough in the Middle Ages, and the Yarmouth constituency was represented by two members of Parliament until 1832.

Until the building of the Castle regular raids on the Island by the French continued, and in 1544 the town of Yarmouth was reputed to have been burned down. Legend has it that the church bells were carried off to Cherbourg or Boulogne.

Yarmouth Castle was built in 1547. It survives, and is now in the care of English Heritage. It is effectively a gun platform built by Henry VIII to strengthen the Solent and protect the Isle of Wight, historically an important strategic foothold for any attempted invasion of England.

There is a monument to the 17th century admiral Sir Robert Holmes in the town. In a raid on a French ship, he seized an unfinished statue of Louis XIV of France and forced the sculptor to finish it with his own head rather than the French king's. It can now be seen in St. James's, Church.

Yarmouth Pier was built in 1876 and is the longest timber pier in England which is still open to the public.

Yarmouth Harbour

Above and right
Lymington and Yarmouth Ferry

Wightlink, and its predecessors, has been operating ferry services to the Isle of Wight for over 160 years. From 1796 ferries have been operating across the Solent, linking the Isle of Wight to the mainland. Originally, steam ferries operated a circular route from Lymington to Yarmouth, Cowes, Ryde and Portsmouth.

The rail companies became involved in the operation of the ferries, with individual routes located between Lymington and Yarmouth and Portsmouth and Ryde. Wightlink Isle of Wight ferries now operate a round-the-clock service between the English mainland and the Isle of Wight. A service is run every day of the year on three routes across the Solent and sailings take place up to 230 times a day.

Yarmouth Ferry

Above

A cottage near Newtown in July

Newtown is located on the northern coast of the Isle of Wight between the Medina and the Western Yar rivers. It abounds with buildings of character set in locations of great charm. At one time it was the capital of the Isle of Wight and had a deep and sheltered harbour.

The town was originally called Francheville (ie Freetown) but later the name changed to Newtown. It was probably founded before the Norman Conquest. The town flourished until the French raided in 1377, and with a gradual silting up of the harbour, loss of trade meant that Yarmouth and Newport became the island's principal ports instead.

Right

Causeway Lake at Newtown in September

This tranquil scene offers the opportunity for an interesting walk by the shoreline. The shallow water and half submerged plants create a mysterious underwater environment. There are also many rare wild plants and birds to be seen.

Newtown

Above and right
The Old Town Hall at Newtown

The Old Town Hall is the only reminder that Newtown once had a town as well as a hall. It was built to reflect the status of the island's previous capital before a gradual decline of importance.

By the middle of the 16th century Newtown was a small settlement long eclipsed by the more easily defended town of Newport. A survey in 1559 noted that Newtown no longer had a market and it did not have a single good house still standing. Its harbour slowly became clogged with silt so that it was not accessible to larger vessels.

Elizabeth I breathed some life into the town in 1584 by awarding it two parliamentary seats. However, the two members made Newtown one of the most notorious rotten boroughs. By the time of the Reform Act in 1832, Newtown had just 14 houses and 23 voters, and the seats were abolished.

The Old Town Hall

Above

The view from the Castle at Yarmouth in August

Yarmouth Castle was the last stone artillery fortress built
for Henry VIII, in 1547. With no central tower, the main
rectangular block has a square battery to the front and an
early arrow-head bastion on the exposed angle. Yarmouth is
named for its location at the mouth of the Western Yar river.

Right

*The starting cannon at the Royal Yacht Squadron, Cowes
in August*

The Royal Yacht Squadron is the most prestigious yacht club
in the United Kingdom. Its clubhouse is located in Cowes
Castle on the Isle of Wight. Member yachts are given the
suffix RYS to their names, and are permitted to fly the white
ensign of the Royal Navy rather than the merchant red
ensign flown by the majority of other UK registered vessels
and small craft.

Castles and Cannon

Above and right

Cowes Week fireworks; yachts passing the Needles

When seven yachts signed up for the first organised yacht race at Cowes on 10th August 1826, it is unlikely anyone envisaged that this would become the annual world-class yachting event that we now know as Cowes Week. With over 1,000 yachts and 8,000 competitors taking part in some very challenging first-class sailing, the event attracts a wide range of local, national and international entrants, from true amateurs to Olympic and world champions.

Cowes Week offers something for everyone, with its exciting racing schedule and varied shoreside activities all helping to ensure a unique festival atmosphere and an amazing spectacle.

For a southern spectacle, Cowes Week is probably unique. The sun shines from behind, highlighting a magnificient range of colourful sails, and this racing is skillfully choreographed by the Royal Yacht Squadron and regulated by its cannon. Then, as darkness falls on the final evening, a dazzling pyrotechnic display lights up both sides of the Solent shore.

Cowes Week

Above
At the end of its useful life

Fishbourne is a small village between Wootton and Ryde, on the Isle of Wight. The name 'Fishbourne' might mean 'stream of fish' or 'fish spring.' It is positioned on the eastern bank of Wootton Creek, and includes the terminal for the Wightlink car ferry from Portsmouth.

A suitable place to return to the mainland and head for Portsmouth on the Solent Shore, this Fishbourne should not be mistaken for the location of the Roman Palace on the mainland.

Right
Portsmouth ferry leaving Fishbourne

Fishbourne

Above

Appley Tower in September

Ryde is one of two major seaside resorts on the Solent, the other being Southsea. Its role as the Island's principal ferry port, with frequent train services to Newport and the popular resorts of Sandown, Shanklin and Ventnor, acted as a catalyst for rapid growth during the 1800s. As a dispersal point for the Island's visitor explosion, Ryde became a mirror of Victorian taste. It acquired many interesting buildings: the folly known as Appley Tower that dispensed teas to 19th century gentility, for example. Brigstocke Terrace was singled out specifically by Sir Nikolaus Pevsner. In his seminal *Buildings of England* he described it as a 'monumental' sea-front composition'.

Right

Afternoon tea on the seafront in September

Ryde

Above and right
East Sands in June

Today, Ryde's sands are its glory, but it still remains the focus of fast ferries from Portsmouth and their associated services: the Island Line rail link and the extensive Southern Vectis bus services. At the top of the town, is a conspicuous landmark – the sky-assaulting upthrust of All Saints Church – dating from 1872 and reflecting the work of architect Sir George Gilbert Scott.

East Sands

East Wight

Above and left
Rock pools at St Helens in August

Situated on the most easterly point of the Isle of Wight, lying beneath the headland of Culver, is the village of Bembridge. Once cut off from the rest of the Island, Bembridge was connected by an embankment built in the mid-1800's and since then has grown rapidly, so much so that today it can claim to be the biggest village in the UK. It has a good mix of shops, pubs, restaurants and art galleries, and is a popular sailing centre with a delightful harbour and pleasant beach with rock pools. It is also home to the National Trust Windmill, the only one to survive on the Island. Bembridge Airport is the only hard surfaced runway on the Island, and is open to the public 7 days a week throughout the year.

St Helens lies in a coastal position between Bembridge and Seaview. A short walk down to The Duver, a spit of shingle and sand, will give children the chance to explore the rock pools.

Bembridge is next to St Helens, the two centres sharing a harbour and a host of smugglers' tales. A popular yachting centre, Bembridge is synonymous with a hazardous coastline. As such, it merits one of the Island's two Lifeboat Stations (the other is at Yarmouth). And yet it manages to distance itself from the Solent proper by looking northeastward towards Spithead and the curve of Bracklesham Bay.

Bembridge

Above

Thrift growing on The Duver in June

Growing in dry, sandy, saline conditions, Thrift is a common sight on British beaches and salt marshes.

A Duver (pronounced to rhyme with cover) is an Isle of Wight dialect term for an area of sand dunes. The name has become part of place names on the Isle of Wight, for example Dover Street in Ryde is the street which used to run down to The Duver.

There are relatively few dunes on the Isle of Wight, some having been reclaimed for development and others lost. This means that some places which bear the name Duver are no longer sand dunes. The largest surviving example is this one called St Helen's Duver.

Left

Bembridge Windmill in June

A windmill was built at Knowles Farm in around 1700 and still exists today. Bembridge Windmill is the only surviving windmill on the island and has much of its original machinery intact. Last used in 1913, the stone-built tower with its wooden cap and machinery has been restored and visitors can explore its four floors.

Bembridge is a village and civil parish located on the easternmost point of the Isle of Wight. It had a population of 3,848 according to the 2001 census of the United Kingdom.

Right
Towards Freshwater from Brook Chine

Chines are the remains of ancient river valleys, now mostly small gullies leading down to the sea. The term 'chine' is used only on the Isle of Wight and in parts of Dorset and Hampshire. As the walls of the chines and cliffs of the south coast of the Isle of Wight are so unstable and erode continually, the strata is clearly visible. Chines are therefore very important for their fossil records, their archaeology, and the unique flora and fauna for which they provide shelter .

Freshwater is a village at the western end of the Isle of Wight. Freshwater Bay is a small cove on the south coast of the Island which also gives its name to the nearby part of the village of Freshwater. The Arch Rock was a well-known local landmark but fell down in 1994. The neighboring Stag Rock is so named because supposedly a stag leaped to the rock from the cliff to escape during a hunt. Another huge slab fell off the cliff face in 1968, and is now known as the Mermaid Rock.

With its changing rock and landforms, this is a coast not only of varied beauty but also one of great scientific interest. Due to its accessibility and unique nature, there are considerable pressures from recreation and tourism, particularly during the Summer season. The Tennyson Heritage Coast extends from St Lawrence to Totland Bay along the Island's southern coastline. This wild open coastline of fossil-rich sediments culminates in the towering chalk cliffs at Freshwater Bay. Beyond this are the famous Needles rocks and the multi-coloured sandstone cliffs of Alum Bay. The coast is very accessible from here, with the Military Road alongside and a clifftop footpath following its entire length.

Freshwater

Index